SITUATIONSHIP GURU

Situationship Guru

A FED-UP WOMAN'S JOURNEY THROUGH A SERIES OF FAUXMANCES

Kay Monét

Kay Monét Reeves

First Printing, 2021

Library of Congress Cataloging-in-Publication Data is available upon request.

ISBN 978-0-578-85558-5
ISBN 978-0-578-85941-5 (eBook)

Printed in the United States of America

Cover by Co Creative, Cleveland, OH

DEDICATION

This book would have never existed if it weren't for the countless hours my sister, Janay, spent pouring into me. You allow me to be my authentic self, yet, encourage me to the be person God has called me to be. Thank you for believing in me and constantly reminding me that I'm worth it. I love you. You are my vision board!

Contents

1

THE GARDEN OF EGOS

"The lesson will always repeat itself, unless you see yourself as the problem-not others."
-SHANNON L. ALDER

In the beginning, there were manipulators, timewasters, and those with wandering eyes. You name it. I had entertained them all. I started dating when I was fifteen and had never been one hundred percent single for longer than a couple of weeks since then. Guess you could call me a serial monogamist. Since I'd always jump to a new man so quickly, I never had time to analyze why the previous relationship failed. Guys rarely gave closure anyway, so I deemed it unnecessary to try to figure out what went wrong on my own. It would probably just be a waste of time and prolong a relationship that should have never transpired in the first place. Besides, I was convinced that my ex-boyfriends were the problem, although cycles of past scenarios crept into every new relationship. The repeated failures had to have been a coincidence because surely my being the common denominator in every situation had nothing to do with it, right? Wrong! Unresolved issues built up on the inside of me, and no matter how hard I'd try to hide them, my insecurities would seep out at the most inopportune times. Most of the arguments derived from the lack of time being spent together. Quality time was a necessity for me, so I admired men who could make time for me and despised those who didn't.

Attention seeking had been at my core from a very young age. My father had worked two jobs for as long as I could remember, so my need for heighten attentiveness from the male species developed from childhood and had been on steroids ever since. I didn't realize how bad it had gotten until I graduated from college. Most graduates spend their time sharpening their skills, networking and setting themselves up for success in their future endeavors. Instead of focusing on a career, I spent my time in search of love. Misguided and ill equipped with the necessary knowledge to maintain a healthy relationship, I swiftly found myself trying to navigate the intricacies of a situationship. What started as an innocent encounter would soon unlock a level of vulnerability that would cause me to sell my soul for acceptance.

THE SIGNS ARE ALWAYS THERE

As I reminisce on the relationship that proceeded the one that initiated the tug of war inside me, I can't help but wonder what would've happened if I approached the situation differently. If I would've left, instead of trying to convince him that I was worthy, would I have gotten off unscathed? In hindsight, I should've physically moved on, instead of thirsting for sporadic emotional connections. Doing so could've allowed me to flourish through other relationships with my self-worth still intact. Well, all of the would haves, should haves and could haves won't help me now. The signs were there. They always are, but I pretended the red flags were red carpets, and strolled right into the premier of a sad, yet familiar film. Imagine my surprise when I found out that the leading lady's name was the same as mine, and so were her actions.

DON'T HAVE MIXED FEELINGS ABOUT MIXED SIGNALS

The opening scene consisted of me basically throwing myself at a man who made it painfully clear that he wasn't interested in me romantically. We'd always been cool but when he flirted with me at a social gathering, I convinced myself that we could be more. Him giving me a hug at the end of the night and whispering in my ear for me to meet him at his apartment, sent my imagination into overdrive. It was two o'clock in the morning, so I did what any respectable young woman would do in that situation. I scurried home, shaved, ate some pineapples and put a miniature hoe-on-the-go kit in my purse, before driving to his place. His roommate answered the door. The look on his face insinuated that he knew the walk of shame would be waiting for me the next morning. Unashamed, I asked him to point me in the direction of fornication and with a smirk, he happily obliged. When I got to the room, we embraced and gave each other the look two people give one another right before the bed springs sing. The look said jump in my lap and never leave, but his actions said, goodnight and sleep well. Confused, yet determined to ignore the mixed signals, I tried to give his hand a guided tour of my trail of temptation, but he rejected me. With a puddle of feelings that matched the one in between my legs, I swiftly got dressed in preparation to leave. I was embarrassed. Nothing like that had ever happened to me before so I didn't know how to handle it.

"No. Please stay. I want you here." He objected.

"Stop playing with me!" I growled.

"Ain't nobody playing with you girl". His words were accompanied by a little chuckle, so it was very hard to believe his previous statement.

Maybe he's shy, I thought to myself. Or maybe this is karma for the many men I've pulled the friend card on while lying in the bed next to them. Even though I knew nothing was about to happen, I still snuggled up to him for a night of uninterrupted sleep. Platonic cuddling was like going under the knife with no anesthesia. He woke up refreshed, while I arose with the pain of rejection and the weight of frustration on my shoulders. He let me know that he enjoyed my company but preferred for us to stay friends. Why didn't he want me? Flashbacks of me being isolated all throughout elementary and middle school began to resurface. I couldn't go through that again, so I concocted a plan to make him mine. Since friendship is what he wanted, I gave him that, then eventually persuade him into wanting more. People pleasing, although it was a gift and a curse, was something that I had mastered. When you experience loneliness at the level that I did, you'll do almost anything for someone to keep you company. My goal was to become everything he needed so that one day, he'd realize he couldn't live without me.

NEVER TRY TO CHANGE THEIR MIND

Little by little, my plan seemed to be working. Soon, he had a personal toothbrush and masculine scented soap at my apartment. Not to mention, there was a special section of my grocery list that was solely dedicated to the types of snacks that he liked. In only a short period of time, I had given him the key to my place, and we were spending every night together. There was still no intimacy though. We'd kiss often but that was about it. In his mind, we were still just friends, but for me, I was his boo and I needed his actions to reflect such. He never gave me a key to his apartment, but I convinced myself that it was out of respect for his roommate's privacy. He didn't buy special snacks for me to keep at his house either. The only food I was ever able to find was beer and day-old crackers. All signs were pointed toward the exit, but I remained diligent. Hoping and praying that he'd one day deem me worthy and be proud to call me his. Before my dream could come true, there was an abrupt halt in our fauxmance (fake romance).

We were in graduate school and his organization had a major event lined up that would take several months of preparation. His contributions would be a key factor in the success of the event, so that platonic cuddling that I once despised, quickly became something that I yearned for. Weeks went by where I didn't get to see him. He'd still call, but quality time had become nonexistent. One week, his organization bought in extra help as the event's date was swiftly approaching. Being that he now had extra help, I was sure that he'd be enthusiastic about filling the slight opening in his schedule with a woman's presence. Well, I was right, but in the worst possible way. Instead of coming to my spot to spend the night with me, he decided to link up with the campus's Light-Skin Trend. You know the light-skin girl with long hair and an uncomfortable sized booty that all dudes had on their to-do-list. Yep, that was her! She had bounced her way through plenty of men in his social circle and that night, my man was on the menu. The thing that hurt the most was that he called me while she was in his bathroom getting ready for him. Her seductive voice was the last thing I heard before he rushed me off the phone.

My feelings were shattered into a thousand pieces. Technically, I didn't have the right to be mad because he told me in the very beginning that he just wanted to be friends. Instead of taking his words at face value, I took it as code for try harder. My efforts were in vain because I could never look like her. My cinnamon colored complexion and shoulder length tresses could never be attractive to him. Although my butt could fit nicely into both of his hands, I still didn't seem to be good enough. It was time for the pretending to stop. I had thoroughly convinced myself that we were an item, but the truth choked all of the make believe out of me. I didn't seek closure because I felt it to be unnecessary. From experience, when I confronted men about how they had wronged me, they'd find a way to turn it back on me, so I taught myself to live in silence. He had made his choice and it was time for me to move on. His lack of remorse was apparent when he called me and tried to have a regular conversation. Everything in me wanted to give him a piece of my mind, but he already had a piece of my heart. Giving him dominion over both would have been irresponsible. He continued to call and even came over unannounced, but his key didn't work because I had changed the locks. Slowly, I began to fall back by screening his calls. That may have worked if I didn't torture myself by listening to his voicemails an unhealthy amount of times each night before going to bed. The conflicting emotions were damaging to my spirit, but instead of searching for healing, I searched for a new body to lay on his side of the bed.

DATE SOMEONE WHO ACTUALLY LIKES YOU

It didn't take me long to find someone who was interested, but there was just one issue. My new dude and the old one sort of knew each other. They weren't best friends or anything like that, but they were definitely on a first name basis. Oh well, that was a problem that I refused to adopt as my own. The man that I had been playing house with for several months had clearly gone in a different direction and it was time for me to follow suit. My newest love interest had arranged to meet me at a party, so my homegirls and I decided to go. No sooner than I walked through the door, did I see the other dude that I was still very much hung up on. The Light Skin Trend was sitting on his lap and playing in his hair, while simultaneously punching me in the gut without even touching me. Rushing to the liquor table, I hadn't even noticed that my new boo had entered the scene. He hugged me from behind then he poured me a drink. As we were on our way to sit on the couch a fight broke out in our vicinity. There was always unnecessary drama at off-campus college parties. He moved me out of the way and stood in front of me to ensure that I wouldn't get hurt. He was tall, skinny and clean cut so I wasn't sure if he could fight but his protector mentality was still a turn on for me. Once the scuffle subsided, I threw my arms around him and kissed him to show my appreciation. Someone must have called the police about the boxing match because the party shut down shortly thereafter. It was a good thing too. Our make out session was getting intense and we would've likely ended up in one of the empty rooms, rolling on top of each other while making empty promises.

My newly found personal bodyguard and I held hands as he walked me to my vehicle. The short stroll from the house to my car seemed like an eternity, especially when we walked past the man that my heart wanted, but my brain wouldn't let me have. He was very standoffish toward me and his replacement. My new guy couldn't understand why he was acting so funny, but I knew, and I kept it to myself. We parted with a goodnight kiss and made plans to finish what we started at a later date. Before my girls and I could even hit the freeway, my phone was blowing up. Drunk texts from my old flame cluttered my inbox. A lot of what he was typing didn't make sense, but the fact that he kept calling me by my government name irritated me. That was a different type of hurt because you know someone is really pissed at you when all the nicknames are revoked. He had no right to be mad at me for replacing him the same way he did me, but his alcohol level was way past logical reasoning. I invited him to come over for a face to face conversation. Huge mistake! It took him two hours to get to me. Ride shares weren't popular yet and the State Troopers were out so he couldn't risk getting pulled over. When he finally arrived at my apartment, he rolled his eyes at me then locked himself in my bathroom. While in there, he role played with himself, trying to collect his thoughts for our upcoming conversation. When I heard him pretending to be me, I tried my hardest not to burst out laughing. He changed his voice to try to sound like a woman and everything! I was laughing on the inside but terrified on the outside. We never had an argument before. He'd never raised his voice at me, and I wasn't sure what I would do if he did. When he finally came out my bathroom, he pushed passed me as if I weren't even worth the conversation he had just practiced having. Immediately, tears ran down my face. The thought of being deserted by him a second time was too much to handle.

"Stop acting like you don't care about me!" I sobbed.

"Come here." He sighed. "Give me a hug. I'm sorry."

PAY ATTENTION TO WHAT THEY DON'T SAY

Those were the last words we said to each other that night. We were both too exhausted to deal with the emotions that desperately needed to be hashed out. Instead, we went to bed and fell right back into our previous routine. At that moment my brain and heart were in agreement. They both agreed to settle in our stupidity and never mention what happened with the light skin chick or his friend again. They both vanished as if they never existed. We welcomed each other back into our lives as if we had never left but remnants of his jealously popped up often. He surveilled my every move in hopes that I would not entertain anymore placeholders. All of a sudden, we finally had sex and he asked me to be his girlfriend. Those were the things that I had always wanted from him, but something didn't feel right. My mouth rejected the yes that was praise dancing in my spirit. He was everything

I wanted but I still wasn't sure if I was what he wanted, so I asked him what had changed.

He responded, "I don't want you to be with anyone else."

His statement was honest, yet selfish. Back then I smiled, but now I know I should have skedaddled. What kind of answer was that?! "I don't want you to be with anyone else?" Was he serious? Once the layers of bull were peeled back, I realized the translation of his words were indeed disrespectful. He was basically saying that he didn't think that I was special enough to get anyone else at first, but now that I had proven that I could, he needed to claim me before anyone else did. He was a classic narcissist! His ego wouldn't allow him to set me free even when he knew I deserved better. Shame on me for not peeping game earlier, because once again, the signs are always there. He didn't let me change my relationship status on social media or even tell my close friends that we were together. The same friends that had witnessed him flooding my texts with jealousy, were now restricted from celebrating our happiness. Well, they weren't alone because the minute I said, *I do*, to the relationship, I said, *I don't*, to my well-being.

RELATIONSHIPS SHOULD BE PRIVATE, NOT SECRET

He claimed that he was a private person and didn't want everybody in our business, but the truth was, he just wanted to keep me a secret. He didn't want me to be with anyone else, but never did he once say that he didn't want to be with anyone but me. Even if he had managed to let that lie roll off his tongue, I wouldn't have believed him. The fact that he had side chicks was evident in my thrown off PH balance. I had never had any issues during my yearly wellness check until I started dealing with him. It was clear that he was messing with somebody else, and whoever he had chosen was dirty. Luckily the antibiotics got rid of the bacteria, but I wish there was some medicine I could have taken to get rid of him too. Eventually I caught a break when he moved out of state to attend a different graduate school. Long distance relationships suck so I suggested that we should break up, claiming that I didn't want to be a distraction to his studies. The truth was he was a distraction to my life, but I didn't know how to give up on something that I had basically begged for. He declined my offer to break up, repeating that he didn't want me to be with anyone else. So, he packed his bags and all of my former happiness, threw them in his truck and headed south to attend his new school. Our love disappeared in the huge cloud of smoke his car let out as he drove away. He was supposed to visit every other month, but he couldn't cash in any of his sorry excuses for ticket credits. Phone calls became brief and plane rides were nonexistent. When I expressed my disappointment with our level of communication, he'd curse me out for nagging him and then blame all of his shortcomings on me. Begging to have my needs met became tedious, so I started spending time with another man. It started with innocent phone calls but after we went to the concert that Jay Z used to raise awareness for Barack Obama's Presidential Campaign, I knew that my emotional cheating had gone too far. Now I had a bunch of feelings that I couldn't act on because I was still in a relationship. My boyfriend finally visited during Christmas break and he gave me the best gift ever, a breakup! A part of me was a little sad but the thought of being able to take things to the next level with the other dude immediately lifted my spirits. Unfortunately, my ego was demolished when I found out that I was my side dude's, side chick. The woman he really wanted had become available, so I found myself alone again.

There were so many lessons that I should have learned from that relationship. First and foremost, never chase a man. The night he told me that he just wanted to be friends should have been the last night I entertained the thought of him. Instead, I bogarted my way into his life only to have nothing left to show for it. Secondly, don't ignore red flags. Keeping certain parts of your life private is healthy and necessary, but secrecy is toxic. Any man that wants to keep you a secret does not have your best interest at heart. Lastly, don't run from your problems. When my boyfriend wasn't keeping my attention meter full, I went out and gassed myself up with the emotional connections from other men. The temporary fulfillment was short lived, and I still ended up alone. However, being alone is not necessarily a bad thing. It seemed like the end of the world to me because I have a history of rejection that causes me to hold on to things that I need to let go of. Throughout this book you'll see the vicious cycle that I had created for myself repeated over and over again. All of my situationship woes could have been avoided if I just would have embraced these very important lessons the first time around.

2

EXODUS

"You can't run away from trouble. There ain't no place that far".
– UNCLE REMUS, SONG OF THE SOUTH

With a failed relationship and the final semester of grad school on my plate, it was important for me to get myself together and focus. Several miscellaneous dudes entered my life during that time, but I couldn't focus on any of them because I had stuff to do. Plus, my most recent relationship had caused me to put a slight wall up. Who had time to be chasing a dog only later to find out that he had flees? Not me! The real world was just a few steps ahead of me, so I had no time to waste. My hard work paid off because I successfully completed my last semester and landed a job at the university I had just graduated from. As soon as my ninety-day probation in my new position passed, it was time to celebrate! The Caribana festival in Toronto, Canada was rapidly approaching and that would be my graduation present to myself.

AVOID TUG OF WAR LOVE

The weekend was filled with parades, festivals, and several other events that highlighted the Caribbean culture. The party boats were being heavily advertised so my girls and I got dressed and headed to the docks. The music was great, and the vibe was amazing until the boat started moving. The waves had me feeling a little nauseous, so while my friends were on the dance floor whining to the Soca music, I was off in the corner with my head bowed between my legs. Suddenly, I felt a strong, steady hand rubbing my back.

"Are you okay?" Xavier whispered.

"Do I look like I'm okay?" I said with an attitude while trying not to throw up.

He pulled me up to give me some motion sickness medicine and a bottle of water. When I saw how attractive he was I wished I would've been nicer to him. He stayed and took care of me for the rest of the ride. You know how I feel about men being protectors, so I immediately adjusted my tone. By the time we finally docked, I felt like we had known each other forever. We had so much in common, unfortunately this included our heights. Typically, I would only date guys that were taller than me even if I were wearing high heels. Yet, something about his ginger-colored hair and matching freckles intrigued me. His presence was comforting. I could tell he had a big heart, and something inside of me wanted a piece of it. So much so that I was willing to look past his 5'7 frame to get to it. Once we got back to the States, we realized we lived less than forty-five minutes away from each other. The short travel distance allowed us to spend a significant amount of time together. Since quality time was something I lacked in my previous relationship, I fell for him quick and hard! So hard that I stayed with him even when everything in my body told me to run! There was always something different about Xavier but my infatuation with him made me ignore the red flags. Cleary, I had yet to learn the lessons that I previously laid out. Similar to my last boyfriend, he never tried to move too fast with me, even though I was down for whatever. Worried that he too would try to stick me in the friend zone, I began to pull away, but he never let me go. He told me that he respected me and wanted to focus more on mental intimacy. So, convinced and honored that he had put me on such a high pedestal, I proceeded with saying, *I do,* to a relationship with him. Again, not knowing all the, *I don'ts,* that would follow.

Xavier and I had officially announced our relationship on social media after several weeks of dating. Both our pages were full of likes and congratulations as most of our followers had witnessed him courting me. One of our followers had a captivating point of view of our love story. She sent me a direct message (DM) and asked if we could meet somewhere to talk. She and I were from different circles, and our crews never cared for each other much. I didn't trust her and didn't want to meet with her alone, so I just gave her my number and told her to call me. When she called, I could feel her uneasiness through the phone. She sounded as if she were grieving. Something in me wanted to console her and let her know that everything was going to be okay. Little did I know I was the one that was going to need consoling. With a heavy heart, she told me that she needed to tell me something important.

After a deep breath, she managed to mumble through her tears, "I'm sorry, but your man is on the down-low."

Those words successfully cut off my air supply. All the blood in my head rushed down to my feet. I couldn't move, nor breathe. All I could do was cry and listen. She informed me that Xavier and one of her gay male friends were intimate with each other a few years back. Her male friend ran across our relationship announcement and became instantly offended by my man's attempt to hide his true self. He vented to her, telling her all the details of their dirty adventures, and she, in return, told me. I could've gone my whole life without hearing those details. I blacked out. I don't remember ending the phone conversation and definitely didn't recall getting in my car. Still, I ended up outside of Xavier's dental practice, waiting for him to *come out*. He didn't come out fast enough, so I busted in.

"During all our mental intimacy talks, it would've been common courtesy for you to tell me you like guys!", I screamed.

He was nervous.

"Wait."... Huh? What are you talking about?"

My response was an eye roll so severe that I'm sure he thought my head was going to start spinning next. With eyes full of tears, I started hyperventilating. Xavier tried to comfort me during my full-blown panic attack, but I had a feeling it wasn't for my benefit. He was doing everything in his power to keep me quiet, so his co-workers and patients wouldn't hear our conversation. Refusing to censor myself, I continued to inform him of all the secrets that had just been revealed. He was shaking, but he managed to embrace me while assuring me that none of what I had been told was true. Xavier was a smooth talker, and he knew how to manipulate me by telling me that he loved me too much to ever lie to me. I wanted to believe him, but more than that, I wanted to feel that I was worthy of love. No one else had ever made me feel the way he did. I had become accustomed to the idea of us being together forever, so I made myself believe him. I swept all my feelings and that horrible conversation under the rug and walked around the figurative lump in my carpet for several weeks.

REAL FRIENDS WILL TELL YOU
WHAT YOU NEED TO HEAR

Everything seemed to be back to normal until two of my good friends called me late one evening. At first, I wasn't alarmed by their late-night phone call. They'd often call to give me the scoop on the latest drama. I've never been much of a phone person, but gossip was always much more enjoyable when the stories came in high-pitched enthusiasm. This time was different, though. All the excitement had disappeared from their voices. Something told me that instead of being told about other people's business, this time, I'd have to endure a three-way intervention about my own life. They explained to me that one of them had received a call from a concerned party, indeed giving her the same information that I heard a couple of weeks prior. My former foe had become my frenemy after our conversation and had promised that she wouldn't share those details with anyone else. Just to be sure, I asked a few questions to verify the information hadn't come from her. She wasn't the culprit. Since another source had come forth with the exact same information, it was no coincidence.

The truth was being shoved down my throat, but I still denied all the accusations. To protect Xavier, I became very angry with my friends, disrespectful even. They had never seen me like that before. Full of emotion, I unfairly spewed all the pent-up aggression that I should have released on Xavier, onto them. Protecting him was negatively impacting my character. My friends didn't appreciate my attitude, so they ended the call, and later ended our friendship as well. This secret had now cost me my friends, my self-respect, and I risked losing the love of my life. Multiple sources knew the truth, and deep down in my heart, I think I did too, but I wanted to give our love a chance. He knew the best and worst parts of me, but he accepted me anyways. The least I could do was believe him, so I tried my best to do so.

DON'T LOVE THEM MORE THAN YOU LOVE YOURSELF

The next chapter of our relationship was a blur. Although it was very selfish, I finally understood why my ex would tell me that he didn't want me to be with anyone else. Now more than ever, I obsessed about Xavier spending every idle second of every day with me because I wanted to make sure he wasn't spending it with other people, men specifically. I found it very interesting that he was an orthodontist, but for some reason, he couldn't fix his mouth to tell me the truth. My hunger for honesty began to annoy him, and I was annoyed by his anger. There I was, trying to love him through my pain and accept the past that he was unwilling to share with me, yet he had the nerve to be annoyed with me? Our relationship faded quickly, but my love for him remained. To this day, I still care about his well-being. I almost refrained from sharing this story in fear that my truth would negatively impact his way of life, and I wanted to protect him. But who would protect me? If I were ever to obtain substantial healing, the real root of my issues needed to be exposed.

We eventually went our separate ways but just like in the past, I never really received closure. Was he really on the down low or had several people, from several different walks of life, created an elaborate plan to play a cruel joke on me? Perception is reality, but my reality was that I loved him no matter what and didn't really want to believe what I believed. After we broke up, I took a hiatus from relationships. The serial monogamist in me felt the need to latch on to any guy within a five-foot radius but after that situation with Xavier, singleness was deemed unavoidable. Getting dumped by my secret ex-boyfriend was one thing. Being pushed to the side by my side dude was another, but this whole Xavier thing was a new level of discomfort. We've all heard preachers say, "Don't talk to God about how big your problems are, talk to your problems about how big your God is." I knew this experience was somehow a part of the Almighty Father's plan for me, but if any other route were available, I would have definitely signed up to take it.

The enemy's plan was succeeding at a rapid rate, and my faith in God was dwindling at the same frequency. My emotions were hard to articulate so I sought after a professional to help me navigate my feelings. If I kept holding everything in, I would eventually deteriorate. Xavier was usually there to listen and help me brainstorm whenever my life had gotten off track. Now that he was gone, there was no one there to show me what to do. Plus, I was too embarrassed to talk to any of my friends about the situation. Most of my friends knew him and, to keep him safe, I kept my mouth shut. Thankfully, my job's Employee Assistance Program (EAP) offered three free counseling sessions. My counselor didn't understand me the way I needed her to though, so I never went through with all of my sessions. Therapy is now more widely accepted in the African American community, but there was a time when it was frowned upon, especially by the elders. "Black people don't need therapy because we have God" was one of the many myths that I had to struggle through to even sign up for help. So, when I finally did, I needed someone who would keep it real with me. Someone who had a similar background that I could relate to. My counselor was nice, but I could tell that she grew up on the right side of privilege and would be unable to empathize with my upbringing. That's why I was always so frustrated when she wanted to talk about my childhood. Granted, most cognitive behaviors stem from something a person has gone through as a child, but we only had three sessions. Spending all of the allotted hours digging at the root of the issue would have been beneficial, but my most recent tragedy had broken every logical bone in my body. Instead of doing the work to get healed, I ran away from the solution like I had always done.

My pain was pushed way back into my subconscious with hopes that no one would ever find it, especially not me. In time, I became numb and pretended like that part of my life didn't happen. Typically, when a woman experiences heartache, she does something drastic like cuts her hair, or self-medicates with drugs and/or alcohol while destroying the man's personal belongings. Well, it was going to take more than a new hairdo and a bonfire full of his clothes for me to tackle the obstacles that were in front of me. Finding out that the so-called other woman that is wreaking havoc on your relationship was actually a man, causes a different type of shame to attack you. Feeling like an outcast, I decided to pack my stuff and leave the only place I've ever known to travel to unfamiliar territory. My last relationship tried to teach me not to run from my problems, but I seemed to be a repeat offender and had to learn the hard way.

Operation Get the Hell Out of Dodge was in full effect! Every waking hour of every day was spent trying to come up with an evacuation plan. Humiliation and disappointment oozed from the holes that had been poked in my confidence. Yet, I slapped on a fake smile and muddled my way through life. I'd often use apps to enhance blemishes on my photos, but there was no filter that could cover my emotional scars. I was in danger of being exposed. Pretending like nothing was wrong was eating me alive. My lack of interest in myself, social activities, and life, in general, was beginning to raise concerns. People questioned me left and right, to which I continuously gave vague answers. It was funny how my ex's failure to come out of the closet forced me to push my truth in the proverbial closet as well. I couldn't tell people that the man I planned to spend the rest of my life with was bisexual. If he didn't even want me to know his true self, I'm pretty sure he didn't want my nosey friends and family to know either. So instead of telling them the truth, I gave them some heartbreaking story about how I felt like my life had become mundane, and I needed a change. It was a true story. My dark and dull routine had become scary to watch. I had to do something, and I had to do it fast!

The only reason why I hadn't moved immediately after my relationship ended was because I wasn't sure where to go. My issues with loneliness prevented me from moving to a place where I didn't know anyone. Suddenly, I remembered that my friend Jade, lived in Atlanta, Georgia. God must have aligned our paths because she was actually looking for a roommate. My new hiding spot was now secured! The next day I gave a resignation notice to my employer and started making plans to uproot my life and plant it in a new city. Everything happened so fast, and I hardly weighed the pros and cons of my decision. Was I scared? Of course, but if I would've waited until I got all my ducks in a row, I might not have ever left. Michelle Obama said, "You can't make decisions based on fear and the possibility of what might happen." So, I just put on my big girl panties and started making moves.

Now that I had a relocation destination, it was time for a mental overhaul. Since I never completed my EAP healing sessions, my issues remained unresolved. Honestly, I wanted a time machine so I could forget everything that happened and just start over. I wanted to disappear into thin air, but the longing to feel sexy was more potent than my desire for amnesia and invisibility. My self-esteem was at an all-time low. My recent role as Xavier's Cover Girl didn't exactly have me feeling easy, breezy nor beautiful. I dove headfirst into a promiscuous lifestyle in hopes that my erotic activities would lend themselves to fulfillment in other areas.

SEX ONLY TEMPORARILY NUMBS THE PAIN

Since I lived in a college town, the prospects were either inexperienced or illegal. Venturing out to neighboring cities in pursuit of pleasure became my nightly occupation. One night, my girls and I went to an upscale lounge where I saw a familiar face—Tobias. The last time I saw him was during our junior year of college. In all those years he hadn't changed a bit. He was handsome and well-dressed. His goatee that perfectly framed those big, juicy lips was just as appealing as it had always been. While in college we both had reputations. Mine was for being a good girl as many of my relationships were lowkey. His, however, was for being a whore because all his sexual encounters were basically advertised as front-page news. We often addressed him as the "Campus Loop", which was a nickname derived from the college shuttle bus that stopped at every dorm at the university.

During college, I was shy and inexperienced. Now, I was brave and wanted to know if the rumors were true. I wasn't as experienced as he was, but I was eager to learn, and I wanted him to be my teacher. Tobias smiled at me, and I melted right there in the middle of the dance floor. He grabbed my waist, pulled me close to him, and we proceeded to slow grind to every song. There were no words, just movements—suggestive movements. My hips were holding a full conversation with him, and he was fluent in my body language. Our lips touched, and our tongues followed. We parted ways that night, but surely that wouldn't be the last time I felt his body close to mine.

Tobias was the type of guy that made me want to take my panties off and hand them to him with no questions asked. He was incredibly sexy, and I hoped that my underwear would be unnecessary during our next encounter. Fantasizing about all the ways I would explore his body became the best part of my day. Imagining his big, rough hands, grabbing me and pulling me closer to him continuously put a smile on my face. He had calluses on the palms of his hands from lifting weights. Oh, how I wanted him to bench press me. We didn't exchange numbers that night, but I passed my digits to him through a mutual friend. There I go chasing a man again. Oh well, I wanted to feel better and he was just the right man for the job.

We skipped the small talk and he sent me his address. Full of thirst, I pulled up to his place within a matter of minutes. Playing hard to get wasn't even an option. As soon as he opened the door, we rushed to each other as if we hadn't seen each other in years. Our clothes fell off immediately. His chest, arms, and abs were reminiscent of a my-size action figure. Tobias proceeded to fold me up like origami pieces that night. It was what I needed. The ability to have sex without emotions or expectations was a liberating experience. I didn't have to worry about what he thought about me, what others thought about me, or how I felt about myself. It was freeing. He was now my Prozac, numbing me from my past's pain. He numbed me up so well that I became completely oblivious to all the things I needed to take care of before the big exodus.

My notice of separation was already in the hands of my employer's Human Resource department. Conversely, other important things like scheduling an appointment to donate my furniture to charity and finding a successor for my praise dance ministry fell through the cracks. Did I fail to mention I was a spiritual leader at my church? Does that surprise you? It's okay, it still surprises me too. If my former pastor knew I was living in sin, he would've stoned me in front of the congregation as if we were living in the Old Testament. But God wasn't through with me yet, and we have all fallen short of the glory of God. That's every sinner's favorite line to say when they aren't living right. I've used the Roman 3:23, get out of sin free, excuse several times.

Now I was the first to admit that my walk with God had been mighty crooked, and I needed a construction worker to fix the potholes on my path to righteousness. Unfortunately, I wasn't gung-ho to make the necessary steps of correction yet, because truth be told I was still a little salty with the Savior. A significant amount of time had passed since the mayhem with Xavier, but my wounds were still hemorrhaging. Why did the Lord make me go through that, and go through it alone? He could've at least given me a heads up. Having sex was my way of rebelling against Him. I knew I wasn't fulfilling the purpose that He had for my life, and I figured there was no point in trying. He wasn't doing what I wanted Him to do, so I decided to be petty and do the same. I had run away from God just like I ran away from all my other issues.

Trying to live my life without God became overwhelming. Jade knew I was struggling with something, but she didn't know exactly what. I told her a little about the situation but didn't want to overwhelm her with my drama. No one likes a Debbie Downer, especially one with whom you are prepared to share a living space. Jade was a believer as well, so she had selected a few churches in the greater Atlanta area that we would visit once I moved. Her efforts were truly appreciated, but I wasn't sure I was ready to participate in corporate worship yet. Not being connected to ministry was saddening to me but my lack of faith preventing me fully caring.

KNOW WHEN TO LEAVE

My going away party served as the perfect distraction to help me hop out of my feelings. Several people showed up to wish me farewell. It was touching to know so many people cared about me. I contemplated staying, in hopes that my support system would help me work through my internal battles. The only problem was that I was not ready to share the truth with any of them. My friends would be unable to provide guidance if I were unable to introduce them to the problem. Should I stay, or should I go? I played all the possible scenarios out in my mind until the anxiety became unbearable. It was nothing a few shots of liquor couldn't cure. Luckily, my friends were buying several rounds of temporary pain relief. Thus, I was able to get through the rest of the night without a care in the world.

From what I can remember, my going away party was epic, but so was the headache that appeared the next day. I woke up drunk and felt like I had been run over by the U-Haul truck stationed outside of my apartment. Also, I couldn't decipher whether my legs felt so sore because of my twerking or the personalized farewell session that Tobias gave me in the party venue's bathroom stall. Either way, I needed to get my life together. As I struggled to stop the swirl in my head, I realized I only had fifteen minutes before the charity truck would arrive. After the truck carried away my belongings, I sat in my one-bedroom apartment alone. As I began to scroll through my phone to review the videos and photos from my party, I sobbed. Tears continued to flow as I realized I wouldn't see some of my friends again for a very long time. The sounds of my sobbing echoed throughout my empty apartment. I finally gathered up enough strength to walk to the restroom to wash away the raccoon eyes caused by the previous night's left-over mascara. As soon as I entered the restroom, I began to cry even more. What was wrong with me? I was getting ready to embark on an exciting journey. That should have made me feel on top of the world. Instead, I felt like the world was sitting on my shoulders, and my lack of stability, as well as upper body strength, would again prove me to be a failure.

As the remnants of my past's insecurities began to resurface, I realized that those free counseling sessions were worth exactly what I paid for them—nothing. There I was, aimlessly wandering around in the wilderness I had created in my mind, trying to glue the broken pieces of my life back together. My desire to flee from the Midwest was reminiscent of the children of Israel's need to escape from Egypt. At first, I couldn't understand how an eleven-day journey turned into forty years of bondage. Then I realized it was probably the same way my unhealthy six-month relationship with Xavier, turned into several years of settling and cycles. Because they complained, the process of leaving their current situation and excelling to the promised land was prolonged. My goal was never to repeat the fate of the Israelites, but neither God nor anyone else, should have expected me to serve my time without exhibiting a little bit of an attitude. If you found out that your knight in shining armor preferred a cape made of glitter, you'd be a little testy too! I knew complaining wouldn't make anything better, so I continued to bottle up my feelings. Besides, I felt as if no one would have cared to listen to me anyway. In silence, I placed my luggage as well as my emotional baggage in the U-Haul and prepared to transition to the next phase of my life.

3

THE PROMISED LAND

"Go from your country, your people and your father's household
to the land I will show you."
– GENESIS 12:1, NIV BIBLE

After a nine-hour drive full of lane switching, snacks, and my GPS's horrible sense of direction, I finally made it to Atlanta. Sitting in the car for several hours was lonely, so hearing a few familiar voices along the way significantly helped reduce that feeling. When I wasn't on the phone with my loved ones, I alternated between listening to gospel and R&B music. Some type of noise was surrounding me during the whole trip. The slightest bit of silence would've allowed me to ponder my life's choices, which was something I had been avoiding. The fear that I could've possibly made the wrong decision had been haunting me for several days leading up to the move. Turning around and driving back home would have been a strong possibility if I had allowed the silence to settle in for too long. The noise protected me from doubting myself, which was something I did all too often. Luckily, I was only a few exits away from my new apartment when the volume of my thoughts began to increase. There was no turning back now because I was almost there.

UNRESOLVED ISSUES WILL FOLLOW YOU EVERYWHERE YOU GO

So grateful to finally arrive in ATL, I jumped out the car and ran to meet Jade. She had food and wine ready for us which is something that I could get used to. We hadn't seen each other in several years so there was so much that we needed to catch up on. We talked about everything except what I really needed to vent about. She knew I was avoiding the subject, so she didn't force me to talk about it. That's what I loved about her. Her just being there made everything better because I was no longer alone. I picked Jade's brain about Georgia's job market and the social scene. She informed me that there was always something to do in Atlanta and that she had scheduled a few events for us to attend during the upcoming weeks. That was so exciting! I hadn't felt like myself in a while, but things were finally starting to look up.

DON'T BE A REPEAT OFFENDER

While Jade and I were finishing off the bottle of wine, Kourtney texted me, asking if I made it to his city safely. Kourtney and I met at a wedding in Atlanta about a year before I relocated. He had been staring at me all night but never made a move until the very last minute. He cornered me at the coat valet and asked me if he could walk me to my car. We exchanged numbers and social media contacts. He was diligent in his seductive pursuit of me, but our flirtatious conversations ended once Xavier came into my life. Kourtney tried to keep in touch while I was in a relationship, using the cliché tag line that we could just be friends. Determined not to get caught up in emotional cheating again, I didn't entertain any of Kourtney's advances. His number was saved in my phone for a rainy day though. It came in handy too, especially since Hurricane Xavier came through and destroyed life as I had known it. Several of Kourtney's photos caught my attention in the weeks leading up to my move, so I hit him up and asked if he'd be willing to show me around town once I arrived. Truthfully, I couldn't care less about seeing the sights. I was more interested in taking a tour of his bedroom.

Although Tobias and I didn't spend a significant amount of time together, he did teach me a few things and I was eager to share my new talents with Kourtney. Somehow, sex had become my best friend. Sex loved me! She helped my lovers and I achieve our biggest goals. She knew my secrets and only shared them with those I had deemed worthy. Of course, she would also get me into a lot of trouble from time to time. But how could I stay mad at her? My value and self-esteem were wrapped in her essence. She provided me with a level of satisfaction that I was unable to maintain without her. That satisfaction was sure to come with a price though, so I had to be careful.

Everything in me wanted to show Kourtney all of my new tricks but I didn't. He had just gotten out of a serious relationship and I didn't want to take advance of his vulnerability. Plus, I had already experienced being an unsuspecting side chick once before and didn't want to end up in that position again. We were both on the rebound, so any connection we made was sure to lead to multiple headaches. Those were problems that I didn't want or need in my life, but I'd be lying if I said I wasn't curious about his lovemaking skills. Some of our conversations were sexually explicit and I wanted to know if he was all talk. Details of all the things he said he would do to me if the occasion presented itself were always at the forefront of my mind.

DITCH THE DÉJÀ VU

Kourtney's post break-up situation reminded me of one that I had previously been in. I used to talk to this guy that had just broken up with his girlfriend of two years. He told me that he wasn't interested in a real relationship with me. At first, I was offended. Why didn't he want to be in a relationship with me? Did he think I couldn't compare to his ex? Then I remembered what happened the last time I forced a relationship on a man and decided to stay in my lane. Our interactions would be purely physical, and I had to be okay with that. Well, a month or two into our situationship, he began to catch feelings. Instead of coming over just for sex, he began taking me out on dates and wanting to have real conversations. A normal girl would have appreciated his gestures, but it's clearly been established that I'm not normal. In the beginning, I played along but after he released prematurely during one of our sexual encounters, I had to get rid of him. To add insult to injury, he tried to make me eat cereal instead of going over my best male friend's house for brunch one day. In what world would his stale corn flakes ever be better than my homeboy's blueberry pancakes? He had lost his mind and that was the last straw! His one-minute performance and jealousy were considered acts of terrorism, so he had to go!

Trying to avoid the same scenario from playing out with Kourtney, I ignored him for as long as I could, but he was persistent. He had waited months for me to finally move and now that I was finally there, he wasn't going to give up. Kourtney eventually wore me down and I allowed him to come see me. Temptation showed up unannounced about an hour before he was scheduled to arrive, so I scurried to the rest room to pleasure myself and take the edge off. My roommate was sound asleep in her bed so there was nothing but space and opportunity for Kourtney and me to become better acquainted. At first, we sat on opposite ends of the couch, flirtatiously joking around with each other. Later on, we moved from our respective ends and met in the middle for the world's most intense make-out session. My lady parts were pulsating. I was thankful that I got off before he got there because if I hadn't, I might have been in trouble. My lips were chapped from their constant intertwining with his. I rubbed my hands through his dreadlocks while suggestively pressing myself up against his muscular body. Somehow, we managed to break free from each other's spell long enough for me to put myself in time out and tell him that I was ready to go to bed. Luckily, he was a gentleman and didn't take my saying that as an invitation for him to join me. He managed to behave himself that time, but I had a feeling he wasn't going to let me get away that easily again.

AVOID ATTRACTIONS TO DISTRACTIONS

Kourtney was a beautiful yet unwelcomed distraction. I couldn't give him too much of my time because finding a job was my number one priority. I started applying for jobs weeks in advance before I moved to Atlanta, but I still hadn't landed a position yet. The headquarters for several prestigious corporations were housed in Atlanta, Georgia. I got my hopes up for multiple positions, but unfortunately, I kept coming up short. At one point, I even received a notification that my application for an accounting position at a fast food joint had been rejected. How does that even happen? I mean seriously! Fast food was supposed to be the go-to job when you're searching for employment. The corporate offices held individuals to higher standards, but I never imagined getting denied by an establishment that had a drive thru. If you looked up the word defeated in the dictionary, you would find a picture of me sitting on a pile of rejected applications while binge eating French fries. The necessary skill set for this position required a

Master of Business Administration, which I had, so I wasn't sure what led to their decision not to hire me. My pride wouldn't let me call them to ask why they didn't want me, so I dusted myself off and kept it moving.

REJECTION COULD ALSO BE GOD'S PROTECTION

Finding a gig was a necessity but my job searches significantly decreased after receiving multiple rejection letters. My inability to find a job made me feel severely unqualified and insecure. Those emotions were all too familiar. I spent most of my days trying to fill the voids in my spirit instead of filling out applications. One reason I had a hard time searching for employment opportunities was that I didn't know my passion. I'd ventured out on a few different projects, but nothing stuck with me. Several years ago, I tried to join the fashion industry and decided to start my own shoe line. Sadly, after being scammed by the distributor and constantly struggling to find a reliable supplier, I lost hope. They say the dream is free, but the hustle is sold separately. Alas, I didn't have enough coins or confidence to purchase the hustle, and unfortunately, life didn't have a layaway plan. Instead of trying to keep my dreams alive, I tried to keep up with the Joneses and fit into the cookie-cutter image that my new city encouraged. Atlanta, better known as Black Hollywood, appeared to suffer from identity deprivation. Many of the women seemed to look alike, and I was an outlier. I awoke daily to apply a full face of makeup and curled my hair to perfection. No matter how put together I thought I was, I still felt like my weave would never be long enough nor my booty plump enough to receive their stamp of approval. To avoid the disappointment of not fulfilling my dreams and the standards set by Atlanta's most elite circles, I would often suppress my sorrows with shots of liquor. Then I would chase it with dangerous connections with unhealthy people, like Kourtney.

Originally, I vowed to stay away from him, but I became fonder of him as each day passed. The physical connection was still placed on hold though because I didn't want to repeat my previous fate. The more we progressed, the harder it became for me to keep my hands to myself. Kourtney grew on me. I enjoyed his company, but more importantly, I enjoyed the security. He understood and accepted me, so I felt like he would always be available. Some days, I was willing to risk it all to be with him. Throwing all caution out the window would be dangerous, but I felt like he would have been worth it. Then I'd remember that we were both broken. If we would have tried to find our wholeness in one another, we'd both end up in a far more broken state than we already were. The healthiest decision would be for us to just remain friends. Besides, if I spent a significant amount of energy on him, he'd just be another obstacle distracting me from my purpose. I was doing just fine getting in my own way, and I didn't need anyone's help to prevent me from living the life the Creator had planned for me.

The stress of dodging Kourtney as well as dodging the embarrassment of being unemployed began to take a toll on me. Being broke made being single worse. Running out of gas on the way to a table for one tends to alter one's mood. I needed a temporary relief from the stress that was overtaking my soul. The liquor store wasn't open yet, so I did the next best thing—retail therapy. I ventured out to Lenox Mall with hopes of coming home with a new pair of shoes and possibly a new man that could distract me from Kourtney. It quickly became evident that my newly purchased six-inch heels would be the only thing I would take home later that evening. Most of the men at the mall didn't seem to be interested in women. None of them were looking my way. I was quickly able to point out who was straight and who wasn't. Silently, I asked God why He couldn't have given me that gift a tad bit sooner, but He told me to mind my business and I respected His wishes. My previous experience would've made most people homophobic, but for me, it didn't. My attitude was not directed at the LGBT community.

The scrutiny and violence that some members of that society experience were painfully unfair and extremely unnecessary. My problem was with an individual that chose to hide his true self and drag me along for the toxic ride.

BEWARE OF COMFORT FOODS AND COMFORT ZONES

Still in disbelief of what I had gone through, I felt a knot begin to form in my throat. My pride wouldn't allow me to cry in a public place, so I rushed to the food court to eat my feelings. There were several healthy food options that I should have chosen, but I went straight for the fat people food. Emotional eating had always been an issue for me. The calories seemed to calm my nerves. Ever since I was a kid, I would stuff myself as soon as I began to feel sad. Now the little girl living inside of me, was doing what she had always done to try to survive. Just like pizza was my comfort food, toxic relationships seemed to be my comfort zone. Sometimes I wish men came with nutritional labels just like packaged food. You ever notice how the tasty looking foods have some of the worst ingredients. Some of my favorite foods are the major cause of diabetes and other health related diseases that have plagued our community. Just like some of the fine men who seem to have it all together on the outside have caused generations of pain. Yet and still I craved it because it was familiar. I had convinced myself that being in a relationship, no matter how detrimental to my mental and sometimes physical health, was better than being by myself.

Determined to find a new boo and forget about my past, I took matters into my own hands and created a profile on a popular free dating app. The attention that I received was overwhelming, but my matches were unimpressive. They were cute but by the end of the chat, I could tell that they were only after one thing. Once they got that thing they would bounce to the next babe and take a piece of my self-respect with them. I wanted them to at least pretend as if they were serious about getting to know me, but they were uninterested in the extra work. This app allowed these men to be what they truly were which was trash! I should've been grateful that I was introduced to their true intentions instead of their representative, but I wasn't because I still felt empty.

Depression started to set in, and I felt defeat slowly brewing in my spirit. Kourtney could tell I had been distant, so he hit me up to see if we could spend some time together. He had successfully been shipped to the friend-zone but had been doing everything in his power to make sure that wasn't his permanent address. Jade had already invited me to a house party, so I had yet another excuse to decline his advances. I did miss him though, so I allowed him to stop by before we left. He was enjoyable to be around. He whispered several reasons in my ear why I should spend the night with him. They were all very tempting, but I had already promised Jade I would hang out with her and I didn't want to be one of those friends who didn't keep their word. With a quick hug and a kiss on the cheek, I sent him on his way.

ALWAYS LEAVE THEM WANTING MORE

Once my distraction had left the premises, Jade and I hopped in her car and rolled out. Her friend, Bryce, lived close, so he carpooled with us to the party. There was only one word to describe Bryce—yum! His light hazel eyes and matching complexion were pleasing to me, and his cologne ignited my senses. We pre-gamed at his apartment for a while before heading to the party. After a few minutes of us being to-gether, I could tell there was a mutual attraction. Jade stayed in the living room while I followed him to his bedroom to watch him finish getting dressed. He took his shirt off to reveal his eight-pack, v-cut abs.

If he had decided to go to the party shirtless, I wouldn't have been mad at him. I sat on the edge of the bed, contemplating whether I should text Jade asking her to go to the party without us. Suddenly, my mom texted me something God-related that abruptly killed my libido. God always snitches on me to her, so she must have known I was up to no good. Bryce sat on the bed next to me and began rubbing my thigh. Annoyed by my mother's untimely blocking, I flirtishly grabbed his hand, wrapped it around my waist, and escorted him back to the living room.

We finally headed to the party, and by the time we got to our destination, I was feeling a little special. That feeling quickly faded away once I found out that all the compliments and energy Bryce was giving me were far from being exclusive. He was a flirt and a good one at that. It was evident by the smiles that he put on all the girls' faces that night. I was a flirt, too, so his actions didn't necessarily bother me. Especially since a few other guys were charmed by me that night as well. After my crew took their rounds of shots, we decided to head to some local bars. We linked up with two other gentlemen along the way. One of them showed his interest in me and began to pursue me for the rest of the night. His name was Isaac. He was a Systems Analyst for one of the elite information technology firms in Atlanta. He was talking nerdy to me all night, and even though I didn't understand most of his geek-speak, I didn't mind listening. He used the crowded line as an opportunity to get close and accidentally rub up against me. I had no complaints. A few other guys were checking me out that night, but Isaac continued to fight for my attention. When we finally got inside the bar, I couldn't seem to keep my booty off him. Twerking had become one of my favorite hobbies, and the dance floor has always been my natural habitat. After dancing with me all night, he whispered in my ear, trying to convince me to leave with him. Although talks of calling a taxi and going to grab food sounded enticing, I thought it was best that we stayed with the group. Besides, it was about four in the morning, and nothing holy nor acceptable happened during those hours.

About an hour later, we all arrived back at Jade's friend's apartment. The crew went their separate ways. Jade, Bryce and I were still drunk so driving back home was completely out of the question. Jade slept in the bed with her friend, leaving Bryce and I with the tasks of finding a place to rest. He suggested that we share the couch. There was only one blanket, but he promised he would keep me warm. I figured we would just cuddle until we fell asleep, but he had other plans for me. He called himself being jealous that I had allowed Isaac to be in my face the entire night. Determined to get me back on his team, he grabbed my ankles, pulled me toward him, and began sucking my toes! Thankful that I had gotten a pedicure earlier that week, I laid back allowing him to continue. Things got a little weird when I heard him unzip his pants. That sound normally turned me on, but this time nervous energy overwhelmed my entire body. He grabbed my feet again and gently used them to massage himself. Normally, I love trying new things sexually, but this provided zero pleasure for me. If I would have liked him, I would have allowed him to continue. Since I had no feelings for him at all, I pulled away. He was disappointed. He kissed me and tried to hop on top of me, but I denied that too. He was annoyed with me, but I was too tired to care.

The next morning was interesting. Mr. Foot Fetish said less than two words to me on the way back to his apartment. He claimed it was because he was sleepy, but I know the truth. He had the nerve to have an attitude that I didn't sleep with him. Sir, I just met you, why would you expect me to?! He was fine though so maybe he was used to a certain type of treatment from women. Well, I wasn't the one he could expect that treatment from. Actually, I was a tad bit offended that he had volunteered me to be in that category. I should've been mad at myself though. My outfit and some of my actions were giving off the vibe that I was easy, so I couldn't really get mad at him. We dropped him off at his place and I never heard from him again, until he began dating an associate of mine. The concept of never chasing a man was finally starting to kick in. I was proud of myself. The old me would've tried to reach out to him but the new me kept it moving. Besides, I was interested in Isaac anyway, so the thought of Bryce quickly became erased from my memory.

4

THE UNHOLY TRINITY

*"I reserve the right to love many different people at once,
and to change my prince often."*
– ANAIS NIC

Isaac had been texting me non-stop since we left each other's presence. I wish I would've spent the night with him after the club instead of playing footsie with Bryce. It was probably for the best though. The sexual tension between us was deep, so if we would have spent the night together, I probably would've ended up pregnant. Isaac didn't waste much time making sure he saw me again. He asked me on a date the very next day. This would be my first real date since I moved to Atlanta and I was super excited about it. He asked if I would like to go to church with him then allow him to court me for the rest of the day. Although God and I weren't necessarily on the best of terms at that time, I still found Christian men very attractive. When I imagined my future husband, I always imagined myself submitting to a Godly man. Still holding a grudge against Jesus for embarrassing me the way that He did, I declined Isaac's church invitation, but told him I'd be available later that night. He had communion that morning then took me spiked punch tasting later that evening.

He was my kind of guy. I was happy that he wasn't one of those Christians that looked down on others for having a sip or two. We definitely wouldn't have gotten along if he were, because I had become accustomed to having a drink every night before bed. As much as I drank, my tolerance should have been significantly higher than it was during our date. Three spiked punch tastes later, my tipsy behind was in the corner having a dance battle with myself. One of the punches reminded me of the beverage my Granny makes for us during the holidays. She is not slick. I had a feeling she was putting more than just pineapple juice in there.

DECIDE TO DATE DIFFERENTLY

Although I managed to maintain my sexy by not stumbling over my words or my own feet, he could tell that I was feeling the alcohol, so he took me to dinner to sober me up. We went to some swanky Italian restaurant in Buckhead. Apparently, he was fluent in multiple languages and decided to greet our waiter in his native language. Then he had the nerve to pay for dinner as well as pay attention. That's when I realized that I had been cheating myself all these years. The dusty men that I normally dated would have a staring contest with me when the waiter bought the check to our table. Some would suggest that I pay half, while others would take care of the bill but complain about how much it was all night. Isaac was different. He wasn't like some of the 50/50 men that I had dated in the past. He let me know that as long as I was with him, I'd never have to pay for anything. My exes had never said anything like that to me. It was a welcomed change. The way he communicated was something I wasn't used to as well. When I asked him questions, he responded with intelligent, well thought out answers. He appeared to be a great guy, but I was easily impressed. Especially since true gentleman had seemed to become an endangered species over the past several years. After dinner, we went back to his place for a nightcap. Two movies, several forehead kisses, and a back rub later, it was clear that I wouldn't be sleeping in my own bed that night. He asked if I wanted some dessert. I assumed he was speaking about divulging himself into my goodies, but he was talking about actual treats. He came out the kitchen with a plate of weed brownies and some almond milk. He was checking off all the boxes because a classy dude with hood tendencies was also something on the check list for my future husband.

Edibles were never enticing to me, but I didn't want to be rude, so, I indulged. We kissed and cuddled after finishing our dessert. We even did some interesting things with the chocolate sauce that I had originally requested to go along with the brownies. Everything was fine until I started hallucinating. Those edibles had me imagining that I had sunk into the ground and God had to create me from dirt just like he did Adam. Isaac couldn't stop laughing at me. That was not how I had imagined our first date at all. That's why I was surprised when he requested my presence again a couple of days later. He promised there would be no drugs this time, so I agreed to come over.

PROTECT YOUR SOUL

Atlanta traffic was the absolute worst, so it took me over an hour to make it to his side of town. He greeted me with a big hug and a kiss. The kiss was sensual and suggestive, but we managed to pull away from each other long enough to eat the meal he had prepared for us. It was getting late, so I decided to spend the night again. We hadn't even made it through the opening credits of the movie before we started caressing each other. My excitement leaked through my laced underwear as well as the basketball shorts that he had let me borrow. One after another, articles of clothing fell to the ground. Our fellowship continued until about three in the morning. My goddess was not as tamed as it needed to be because I purposely didn't tidy up that area in hopes that it would deter me from going all the way. It didn't. He navigated his way through without a care in the world. When we finished, I hopped in the shower to cleanse myself from all my recent impurities. Isaac accompanied me and felt the need to recap the details of our exotic adventure. He chuckled while telling me that he thought I might have stolen his soul. At first, I blushed, but later, I became a little disheartened by the accuracy of his statement. Although he meant it as a compliment, I don't think he fully realized that I indeed had captured his soul. Our souls were now connected in a manner that was displeasing to God, and yet, we still seemed blissful.

Soon all the joy was sucked out of my body because I was nervous about how we would move forward. We had only known each other for a short period of time. Afraid that he might have lost respect for me, I tensed up. When we first started talking, he told me it was hard to seriously date in ATL because most of the women had already been ran through. It was my goal to show him that I was different from other girls. Instead, I showed him that we were indeed cut from the same cloth. Now my self-assurance had shriveled up like sauteed spinach. When we first started dating, I felt secure and had a bunch of plans for our future relationship. Now that I had given it up so easily, my confidence had shrunken. My insecurities wanted me to ask dumb questions like, "So what are we?" and "Where do you see this thing going?". The rule of thumb is if you ever feel the need to ask these questions, you already have your answer. Real men don't play about stuff like that. If he wants you to be his, trust me you will know. Since, I didn't know, it was only a matter of time before he started acting funny. The serial monogamist in me wanted to believe that this time would be different, but I had set the raggedy pace of our situationship the moment I threw my legs over his shoulders. The voices in my head began to bombard me with questions that I had zero positive answers for, so I just went to bed in hopes that my emotions would go to sleep as well.

THEY SHOULD LIKE YOU MORE THAN YOU LIKE THEM

The morning after was a bit tricky. I got up, got dressed, and left his apartment quickly as if I were late to work or something. The look of confusion on his face was priceless because he knew I didn't have a job. He wanted me to stay for breakfast in bed, but I had to leave so I could come up with a strategy of how to maneuver through the rest of this relationship. Isaac texted me to make sure I got home okay. He also told me that he was looking forward to seeing me again that week. We had already scheduled another date before I let him explore my body, but now, I wasn't sure if I wanted to hang out with him again so soon. It was clear that I liked him more than he liked me, and I didn't want to get hurt. The person who has more feelings for the other typically ends up in their feelings at the close of the relationship.

Things would've been so much easier if I made him my boyfriend before sleeping with him. That's where I messed up. Situationships that are super sexual from the very beginning always lead straight to hell! They start with great sex then slowly move into the talking phase maze that few people can escape from. I've never experienced being a hoe in a permanent location, so I didn't have a game plan. Eventually, I decided that I would just go with the flow and see where it went. I had much bigger things to stress out about, like finding a job. The whole time I was frolicking with him, eating drug filled desserts and dishonoring my good name, I should have been browsing job listing and filling out applications. Some of my previous applications had been receiving positive feedback, but until I had a guaranteed salary and an insurance package, I couldn't fully focus on him.

KEEP YOUR OPTIONS OPEN BUT
YOUR LEGS CLOSED

Luckily Isaac was scheduled to go to Spain for a couple of weeks. That gave me some time to analyze things and reevaluate my life. I started to like him more than I should have, so I convinced myself that I needed to date other people concurrently to prevent myself from getting caught up. The same night I met Isaac, I had also met Q. Coincidentally, he was a friend of Jade's friend, so I knew I could arrange a meet up at a later date if I wanted to. He asked for my number, but I didn't give it to him that night because I was technically there with Isaac. That didn't stop me from looking his way a few times though because he looked good! He was tall with dark chocolate skin, and whenever he smiled, I disappeared in his dimples. Q had a strong, square chin that was reminiscent of Superman's. I would volunteer to be his damsel in distress any day. The shirt he wore when we first met still weighs heavily in my memory. It read, "The Legend." The interesting part of this was that there was an arrow pointing down toward his manhood. Legend, huh? I became color blind to the beaming red flag because I wanted to meet the man and the Legend as soon as possible. The feeling must have been mutual because he had been asking Jade's friend about me since we first met. She set up another house party for us to accidentally run into each other again. As soon as we locked eyes, I knew I was in trouble. I have a horrible sweet tooth, and chocolate has always been my choice of indulgence. Q poured me a drink then poured on the charm. I could tell that a woman had never tamed him, and the idea of that challenge inspired me to become the first. That man looked like he would ruin my life, my uterus, and my self-respect without even breaking a sweat. My instincts told me not to trust a man that had one initial for a full name but making horrible decisions seemed to be my specialty, so I proceeded without caution.

"So, what's up with you and that little nerd you were hanging out with the other night? I better not get too close to you because your man is going to be upset." He probed.

With a seductive smile, I said, "Well, my man is out of the country. So, if you won't tell him, neither will I."

ALWAYS AVOID SIDE PIECE SITUATIONSHIPS

The side piece saga continued. We were both unbothered by the blurred lines of commitment. Q didn't care that I was semi involved with another man. He had placed a target on my chest and had every intention of getting what he wanted from me. He also had a flock of females that would always be at his disposal as well. I welcomed the competition, with full confidence that I would come out victorious. After a few drinks, we ended up tasting each other's lips. That level of closeness continued for the rest of the night. I found myself grinding and rubbing on this stranger. He took my hand and moved it slowly down the imprint of his jeans. I felt like the Energizer Bunny because my hand kept going, and going, and going. Different fantasies bombarded my thoughts. It took everything in my body for me not to risk it all with him that night. He whispered in my ear that we needed to go somewhere we could be alone. My suggestion was for him to take me out on a proper date the next evening. I know that wasn't what he had in mind but that was all I had to offer at the time. I was already caught up on Isaac, I wasn't about to be stressed out about two dudes at once. I felt a little guilty for cheating on Isaac, but to protect myself, I had to have options.

THE FIRST DATE SETS THE PACE

The next day Q came to pick me up for our movie date. During the drive to the theater, I realized we were kindred spirits. Q had also just recently moved to Atlanta and was exploring employment opportunities as well. In other words, he was broke and unemployed, just like me. There were several other unfavorable characteristics that we had in common. We both enjoyed being in relationships but our track records for successful ones were below average. I informed him that even though I wasn't capable of being in a serious relationship right now, I still wasn't interested in being number two. Here I was entertaining a man while my main dude was in Spain getting money, and I had the nerve to say I didn't want to be number two! Our relationship started off with foolery so I could only imagine how it would end. Hadn't I learned anything from that whole side dude turning me into a side chick situation? Apparently, I hadn't because I was right back to my same old games.

DON'T TOUCH FORBIDDEN FRUIT

He smirked while giving me his conceded look as if to say, "You'll be whatever number I tell you to be". His cocky confidence drove me crazy and nuts at the same time. I was drawn to him but could also tell that he would get on my nerves soon. I had come across a couple of guys like him before, so I knew he wasn't all talk. The whole point of me dating multiple guys was to prevent myself from falling for one in particular. If I refrained from smashing him, I would have control of everything. Staying away from intimate settings would be my best move, but I was naïve and curious. He was the forbidden fruit to my Eve. I knew this would be an uphill battle since the desire between us was so strong. While we were at the movies, we could barely keep our hands off each other. He pitched a tent in his jeans, and I slowly unzipped his pants and started to relieve him. I could tell he was about to explode soon, so I handed him a few napkins then proceeded with the mission. Right before the big finale, my phone started lighting up and ringing obnoxiously. It was Isaac calling! Several people shifted their focus to us as I tried to silence my phone. Q tried to hide his manhood behind the large-sized popcorn bag, but the bag could barely cover it. Luckily, I was able to turn my phone off before the cop shined his flashlight on us. The whole situation was embarrassing, so we left shortly after the incident subsided. As soon as we got back to his car, he insisted that we hop in the back seat so he could properly relieve himself. As badly as I wanted to submit to his demands, I refused. He tried to convince me to let him take me back to his uncle's house, but once again, I denied his access to me. He assured me that he could make it worth my while, but I declined.

KNOW WHEN TO TAKE THEM OFF THE BENCH

After he dropped me off, I could still smell him. His scent began to intensify my desire to be pleased. I immediately stripped and ran to the restroom to take a cold shower. The shower did absolutely nothing to combat my hormones. Normally, I would've just pleasured myself and kept it moving, but I needed a lot more. That night I needed the real thing. It took everything in me not to call Q and tell him to come back. I had already made a conscious decision not to let him get the best of me. Isaac was still out of town, so I had no other choice but to call Kourtney. He was the third person in the unholy trinity I had created in my dating life. He'd been in the friend zone for several months prior, but I knew he was willing and able to give me exactly what I needed. He was excited to receive my phone call and didn't hesitate to invite me to his place. His invitation was all a part of my plan, so I happily accepted. We cuddled and watched tv until I started passionately kissing him. Kourtney didn't try anything at first because he was used to just kissing me without getting anything extra. We had played cat and mouse game for several months, but soon everything would change. As soon as he realized I wasn't wearing underwear, he snatched my dress off so fast. It's as if he was trying to hurry before I changed my mind. Trust me; I had no intention of changing my mind. My visit had a purpose. He aimed to please, and I thoroughly enjoyed being the object of his affection. When we finished, I went to the restroom to take a hoe bath and wash the hot spots that Kourtney recently tainted. Then I went back to the bedroom to put on my clothes. Kourtney was extremely offended that I was about to leave. He made me put my things down and spend the night with him. I initially agreed because I thought we were going to go for round two, but we didn't. He just wanted me to stay with him so that we could cuddle and talk. I had no interest in either of those things. I had already accomplished my goal and was ready to retire in my own space. But, he did a good job pleasing me, so I thought it was only fair for me to continue providing him with the pleasure of my company. While we were cuddling, he told me not to make plans for dinner the next night because he wanted me to cook for me.

I didn't sleep well that night. Was Kourtney catching feelings for me? The whole come over so I can make you dinner scene looked very familiar. This was exactly how it started with the other dude that had just gotten out of a serious relationship. Nobody had time to get caught up in that type of situation again, so I began to plan my exit strategy. I had originally planned to give him a few more months to enjoy the sensation that is me, but I felt like his feelings would grow at a rapid rate. During one of our phone conversations, I told him that we should end things between us. He joked that I would never be able to leave him, and his good fortune alone. Kourtney was confident in his abilities, as he should have been, but my fall back game was significantly strong. It was nothing for me to exhibit a healthy dose of amnesia toward a man that I was no longer interested in. It was weird because I tended to fall for every guy that I encountered, but when they started showing similar signs of interest, I'd run from them. All those scars from my previous relationships began to resurface. Dodging another emotional rollercoaster was at the top of my to-do-list. If giving men an expiration date or secretly sabotaging all my relationships was what I had to do to stay sane, so be it.

5

FATHER OF LIES

*"You can believe in whatsoever you like, but the truth remains the truth,
no matter how sweet the lie may taste."*
MICHAEL BASSEY JOHNSON

J uggling the unholy trinity was a challenge, but based on my previous history, I was more than qualified to handle them. Isaac was
still in Spain, so that gave me many opportunities to come up with different magic tricks to perform on Kourtney and Q. My ability to perform sensual abracadabra drove men crazy and left them wanting more.
I had to tread softly, though. Any uncalculated move on my part could
result in my infatuation with them or their infatuation with me. Both
scenarios were unfavorable. What started as a fun, stress-free experience quickly turned into smorgasbords of foolery. Although adding
new teammates to my roster was somewhat satisfying, there was also a
hint of uneasiness that came with it. Something deep down on the inside of me was off, but I didn't take the important steps to evaluate myself and make the necessary adjustments. Doing so would've required
me to address my issues and face them head on. Who had time for that

level of adulting? Certainly not me. Something had to give, though, because I often found myself repeatedly dating the same types of dudes that meant me no good. It appeared that I had lost my identity somewhere along the drive from the Midwest to the Dirty South. My recent promiscuous adventures, although pleasurable, were completely out of character for the person I was on the inside. Often, I felt like I was having out of body experiences. Slowly but surely, I was taking on a new persona, both physically and mentally. My push up bra and butt enhancing shapewear were becoming a staple in my daily attire. The thought of liposuction even crossed my mind a time or two, but my lack of funds threw a monkey's wrench in that plan. However, I did manage to scrape up enough coins for hair extensions, false lashes, and acrylic nails. I probably would've bought some fake hips if they were sold at my local beauty supply store. Since I struggled with comparison, I would've done anything to be anyone other than myself. My desire to resemble the other Georgia Peaches was dangerous and unhealthy. In addition to going to extreme measures to change my physical appearance, my mental health was plummeting as well. The same girl that was once a frequent churchgoer, now made frequent trips to the liquor and condom aisles of the grocery store.

Poor Jade. She had to watch me deteriorate right in front of her but couldn't help because I never fully opened up to her about what was really bothering me. She never gave up on me though. Jade picked out church services for us to visit every Sunday in hopes of finding a home church. Sadly, our Atlanta church tour proved unsuccessful. There were no churches that I was able to connect with. Had I fallen so far from glory that I was now unable to feel comfortable around other believers? Truthfully, my light was no longer shining brightly like theirs. Mine was kind of flickering like some of the streetlights in the hood. I needed Jesus more than ever but couldn't seem to bring myself to Him.

My spiritual life was hanging on by a thread but so was my personal life. There were several decisions that I needed guidance for. Should I stay in Atlanta or move back home? Which member of the unholy trinity should I focus on or should I just throw them all away? What types of jobs should I be applying for? Why didn't I feel comfortable at church anymore? All these dilemmas needed to be rectified as soon as possible. Making wise decisions was always a struggle for me since there was always a holy version of me whispering advice in my right ear, while the harlot version occupied the left. My inability to make sound decisions on my own caused me to search the scripture for answers. One of my favorite biblical stories was when Jesus turned water into wine because you know alcohol hits different when it's free. But that story couldn't help me find the answers to any of the questions that needed to be addressed.

DON'T RUN FROM YOUR PROBLEMS

As I continued to search, I came across the story of the Prodigal's Son. The Bible had always been a little difficult for me to understand. Especially the KJV Bible because King James was tripping with his hard to comprehend version. I'd suggest reading Luke 15: 11-32 in the Message Bible because it breaks it down in plain English. For those of you who have struggled with understanding the Bible like I did, I'll paraphrase it for you below:

There was a man that had two sons. His oldest son was a fun snatcher. He was a judgmental prude that never allowed himself to have a good time. The youngest son was the complete opposite. He turned up every chance he got. One day, the younger son's baby mama clowned him for still living with his parents. That was an extreme blow to his manhood, so he told his father to give him his portion of the inheritance. The father knew it was a bad idea, but he also knew that he couldn't live his son's life for him. As soon as the funds were deposited into the younger son's bank account, he moved to Atlanta, because that's where everyone goes to get rid of their problems. He spent all his money on dime bags, strippers and dark liquor. After he realized he couldn't even order from the dollar menu, he headed back home. The father received word that his son was on his way home, so he threw him a party to welcome him back. This pissed the oldest son smooth off. He had always been jealous of the younger son and the special party made it worst. The older son confronted his father by complaining that he doesn't appreciate his loyalty. The father consoled both of his sons by letting them know that as long as they are connected to him, they will always be well taken care of. He also let him know that his love is unconditional so even if they got mad at him and/or decided to leave, he'd always be waiting for them with open arms when they came back.

WHEN GOD SPEAKS, LISTEN

God was speaking. He was letting me know that even though I had been ignoring Him lately, He still loved me and would embrace me when I decided to come back to Him. The passage of scripture should've given me the courage to come boldly to God and ask for forgiveness. Alternatively, I retreated and ran as far away from Him as I possibly could. The Xavier debacle still had me in my feelings. Why on earth would I run back to someone who allowed me to experience such heartache? The Prodigal's Son returned home because it was better than his current situation. For me, anything was better than the humiliation associated with being Xavier's beard. Compared to my previous predicament, my current situation of living in the land of the frauds and the home of the broken was just fine indeed.

MAKE SURE THEY ARE REALLY SINGLE

Once again, I ignored my feelings hoping that one day they would all disappear. Just when I thought things couldn't get worse, I managed to stumble upon Tobias's engagement photos, which were plastered all over my social media news feed. The congratulations in the comments, reposts, and numerous likes, killed me softly as I continued to scroll. Completely and utterly disturbed by this sudden announcement, I deactivated my account. It seemed like every time I logged on to that particular social media platform; I received news that ruined my day. Tobias's news was shocking, especially since it had only been a few short months since our last rendezvous. More importantly, I didn't even know he had a girlfriend. My character hadn't been angel-like, but I would never voluntarily sign up to be a home wrecker. I knew he was very friendly with his genitals, so I expected him to have a roster, but I didn't know it would include a full blown out girlfriend.

IT'S NOT YOUR FAULT THEY WERE UNFAITHFUL

There are so many different types of relationships that this new generation of non- monogamists have created. If he knew he wasn't ready to settle down, why would he make a commitment to her? Suddenly, I realized that I was judging him for doing the same thing that I had done in the past and was currently doing in Isaac's absence. In the past, I showed my lack of commitment by emotionally cheating when I didn't receive enough affection. Now I was entangled with three men, so I needed to mind my business. However, I found myself being judgmental again, wondering if Tobias's fiancé wasn't fulfilling his sexual needs and that's why was entertaining me. How unfair was I to blame the victim for getting cheated on? If Tobias wasn't satisfied in his relationship he should have left, just like I should have done when I lacked attention from my significant other. We were the problems. There was something in us that was causing us to be unfaithful, but instead of dealing with our demons, we became one. Then we dragged innocent bystanders along for the ride. I felt sorry for his fiancé. I hoped that he would adjust his behavior now that he was engaged but I wouldn't bet my life on it. Unfortunately, I was no better. If I ever hoped of having a chance at a functional relationship, I needed to stop getting myself caught up in these types of situations.

FUMBLE THOSE FEELINGS INSTEAD OF CATCHING THEM

Luckily, Isaac came back from Spain the day after I found about Tobias's secret life. He was a much-needed distraction from all the drama that was going. As soon as I picked him up from the airport, we fell right back into sin. We couldn't keep our hands off each other. Though I didn't want to admit it, I kind of missed him while he was gone. There was something about Isaac that fulfilled all my needs, which were previously left void. It was God's job to fill all the empty spaces in my life but since I was mad at Him, I transferred the deed to Isaac. All I ever wanted was to feel important. When we were together, Isaac always made me feel like the most significant person in the room. I felt so alive when I was around him. He was my air, and I needed him to survive. He wasn't the best-looking man on earth, but what he lacked physically he made up for it mentally. He was also very affectionate and most importantly, loyal. Well, at least I thought he was. Our love, or lust, or whatever you want to call it, began to fizzle as Autumn approached. Feeling guilty, I reasoned that maybe he had found out that I was being unfaithful while he was away on business. We weren't officially a couple, but I could understand how he would be upset. Most of my friends continued to believe that everything was still good between us, but the truth was he had been consistently dropping the ball. I threw him a slow underhanded pitch, but he fumbled. I know I referenced two completely different sports, but that precisely portrayed the characteristics of our fauxmance. We weren't on the same page about anything anymore, and sometimes I wondered if we were even in the same book.

Cuffing season was right around the corner and he was right on schedule to start acting funny. I knew this would happen, but it didn't make it hurt less. The incident that pushed me over the edge was when his brother flew in from Jersey to hang out with him. He conveniently forgot to introduce me to his family member that weekend but managed to slide by my apartment at a disrespectful time of night for some private entertainment. As soon as he arrived at my place, I confronted him about not being good enough to meet his brother. His mouth was a pleasurable weapon of mass destruction, so he used that to shut me up. Then he was nowhere to be found for the next week. Convinced that he was no longer willing to put forth the effort, I grabbed my phone to delete his number. He sent me a text just at the exact moment I was about to erase him from my life. It was as though he knew I was about to move on, so he felt the need to troubleshoot the issue. Guys always seem to pop back up when they feel their woman slipping through their grasp. It's so annoying. I knew there was no use in trying to revive a relationship that had already died, but he wanted to talk things out. Communication was not my strong suit. Especially when I knew the relationship was about to be over.

SITUATIONSHIPS SHOULDN'T NEED CLOSURE

Once again, I didn't seek closure. It wasn't a real relationship anyway so what was there to close? Plus, this time I had two back up plans to fall back on. Isaac tried to convince me that he missed me and wanted to talk in person, but I could tell it was all game. He just wanted more sex. We both knew it, but instead of being honest about it, he pretended that his only plan was to mend our broken situation. He refused to tell the truth, and I refused to continue to give my body to him. We were not in a real relationship, and the only way our situation could get better was if he changed our relationship status. The forbidden question, "So what are we?" fell out of my mouth, even though I already knew the answer. Isaac responded by giving me random examples of other couples that never had titles but still had strong connections. His rant equated to monuments of nothingness. Those people have nothing to do with us, so I wasn't sure why he even brought them up. He never provided clarification on our future. Instead, he quickly changed the subject and rambled on about something completely unrelated.

My response was, "Why are you speaking in parables? You are not Jesus, bro!"

He was not bothered by my verbal attacks. It was time for me to walk away, but I ended up staying in the unfavorable situation. Isaac's lack of effort soon overshadowed his promises to do better. Deep down, I knew he was no longer looking out for my best interests, but instead that of his own. Our situationship was falling apart, but my self-hatred allowed me to engage in his lackluster love continuously. Shortly after I accepted the fact that Isaac's and my connection would never be the same, I noticed on his social media that he seemed to be out on a date with his ex- girlfriend. He had mentioned her to me a couple of times, but I was never suspicious because he was always down-playing her. Now that I knew the truth, I wasn't surprised that he had gotten back with his ex. It's a natural impulse to go back to your comfort zone, especially when your main squeeze stops giving it up.

DON'T GET CAUGHT LURKING
THEIR PAGE

Most women have the gift of research. Their ability to analyze a person's social media and compile a file of names, dates and addresses without even breaking a sweat always amazed me. Unfortunately, I never received that gift, so I accidentally exposed my lurking on his page with a double tap and he, in return, blocked me. Wow! Devastated, but prideful, I shrugged it off and pretended everything was fine. After my complicated relationship with Xavier, I had promised myself that I would never get so engulfed in another man that I would lose myself again. I vowed never to put another man's feelings before my own, but there I was, yet again, sitting in a pile of tears wondering who I was and why no one wanted me. Therefore, I had to convince myself that it needed to happen. I filled my head up with a bunch of scenarios of how things could have turned out and forced myself to believe that this outcome was the best one.

Thanksgiving came and passed, and I didn't have a grateful bone in my body. My sense of abandonment seemed to overshadow the fact that I had food on my table and a roof over my head. Christmas was right around the corner, and I had no desire to celebrate our Savior's birth. Nor did I have the money to participate in the season of giving. Perhaps going home to visit family for the holiday would have lifted my spirits. Unfortunately, my lack of funds was compromising my ability to escape life's woes. I didn't have two nickels to rub together, let alone enough money to purchase a trip back to the Midwest. And I couldn't ask my parents because they had already paid all of my fees associated with me being the Maid of Honor at my sister's wedding. The whole situation was so humiliating. I was beginning to regret having moved to Atlanta, blaming everyone except myself for my not so perfect circumstances.

Christmas passed and it was now New Year's Eve. For some reason, I still couldn't get Isaac out of my mind. Several glasses of wine later, I had convinced myself that he was on the other side of town missing me too. He hadn't blocked my roommate from following him, so I used her phone to stalk him. I logged in, hoping to see some sad post about how he had lost the love of his life and was thinking of a master plan to get me back. Instead, I saw him sipping cocktails from pineapples with umbrellas in them, with his girlfriend on the beach. I threw the phone across the room. Her iPhone screen and my heart were both shattered. Now I had to go further in debt to replace her phone, but no amount of money in the world could replace my self-esteem. I was unhappy and bitter, and I wanted him to have a similar experience. He honestly wasn't that physically attractive so I couldn't understand why I had fallen so hard. Guess I wasn't mad because I lost the person; it was what he represented that caused me to feel such despair. He was confident and stable, all the things I wasn't. His absence represented my defeat. Since I was unable to keep such a well-rounded man, I felt like a failure again. I had been searching for acceptance, and when I finally thought I had found it, it slipped right through my fingers. I was tired of not being good enough. The wine was not strong enough to erase memories of Isaac's existence, so I started taking shots of tequila. That didn't end well. The last thing I remembered was throwing up in the bathtub. I guess my drunken brain couldn't comprehend the toilet being only one foot to the left. When I finally arose from the dead the next day, Kourtney was beside me. The floor was sprinkled, ever so irresponsibly, with red solo cups, condom wrappers, and whatever was left of my dignity. He had received several unreadable texts from me that night, so he came over to check on me, but I was too drunk to notice. He stayed with me that night to make sure I was okay. There's that protector thing that I liked again. He was my go-to-boo. No matter what happen, I knew he'd always be there. I hate that I was using him, but it was a mutually beneficial relationship. He understood me which is a gift in and of itself, and I never had to be alone again.

6

UNEQUALLY YOKED

*"God is a God of purpose. He's a God of intentionality. He's a God of
vision and He wants to be involved in every area of your life.
Especially relationships! Because relationships, as you
know will make you or they will break you."*
-TOURE ROBERTS, 5 KEYS TO IDENTIFYING YOUR
SOULMATE

The first six months in ATL were spent navigating three hectic situationships, and it was time that I got myself in alignment. Finding a gig was at the top of the list because my bank account was in the red. My emergency fund had sent out several distress signals, and I was about fifty dollars shy of poverty. Something needed to change soon, or I'd have no choice but to move back home. Loading up my recently financed Hyundai and heading back would eventually become my fate if I couldn't get my cash flow situation handled. I cringed at the thought of crawling back with my fast tail in between my legs. The humiliation from my previous relationship had already rocked me to my core. I couldn't fathom going back to the very place from which I was running away. The idea of a failed relationship and a failed relocation was almost unbearable. I had to pick a struggle. It had to be one or the other, but I wouldn't allow it to be both. So, I pushed my feelings to the side as I had always done and started to devise a plan on how to dig myself out of that financial pit.

ENHANCE THE WAY YOU PRESENT YOURSELF

After a couple of minutes of brainstorming I decided that I would reach out to a recruiting agency to help me win interviews. Apparently, my ability to market myself was subpar, so I decided to solicit help. The agency matched me with an African American woman in her early forties. She was about her business and didn't play games when it came to her work. She carried herself in such a way that exuded excellence. Her confidence stepped into the room before she did, and I could tell I was in good hands. The recruiter was very thorough. She analyzed my resume with a red pen and by the time she gave it back to me, it looked like it had been through open heart surgery. Her recommendations severely improved my resume and made me look like a very attractive candidate. Within a week, I had several interviews and landed a position at one of the top historically black colleges and universities (HBCUs) in the country. The job came right on time because my bank account was on its last leg. The HBCU was in dire need of additional help in their accounting department so I was able to start immediately. With a grateful heart, I showed up to work eager to get started and dressed to impress. It was my intention to wow my manager with my skills, as well as secure a suitor in the process. This university was known for producing very successful black men and I just knew one of them would have my name on him. It was clear that after Isaac and I parted ways, I should've taken some time to be alone. But I was ready to dive back in headfirst without a life jacket nor the proper lessons on how to navigate the waves of life. My experiences with the men at the HBCU didn't quite go the way I saw them going in my head. There were some gorgeous guys at my new place of employment, but they seemed to be more interested in my shoes than they were in me. Refusing to go through the Xavier experience again, I steered clear of all the men in the office. Besides, I still had a couple of non-eligible bachelors on deck who were ready and willing to continuously waste my time. It was a blessing in disguise that my job failed to add any additional men to my already drama filled life. Kourtney and Q were already a handful, so searching for a new dude was truly unnecessary.

CODEPENDENCY DOESN'T EQUAL COMPATIBILITY

Kourtney and I had been entertaining each other on a more regular basis ever since I woke up next to him on that eventful New Year's Eve night. Previously, I had put together a master plan to get rid of him by a certain expiration date. With the recent departure of Isaac, my affection meter was running on empty and was in desperate need of a refill. I tried to steer clear from Kourtney especially since I had promised myself, for the umpteenth time, that I would never get close enough to a man to allow him to play me. Yet, something about his spirit continued to draw me near to him. Somewhere between our vow of non-commitment, we became somewhat codependent on one another. I hardly ignored his calls as often as I did before. In fact, there were days when I actually looked forward to hearing from him and made plans to see him on a regular basis.

Our proximity became dangerous. The sex was good but at one point I genuinely began enjoying his company. The more time we spent with each other, the more he opened up to me. He told me about how he was husky and homely looking when he was younger. I would have never been able to guess by looking at the handsome, well-groomed man that stood before me. A wash board stomach, broad shoulders and long, professionally twisted dreadlocks accompanied his 6'0 stature. There was no way he had ever been fat or unfortunate looking. I found myself empathizing with him as he told his story because I too, grew up as an ugly duckling. Our childhood insecurities brought us closer together all the while tearing us further apart. Although we had both grown up to be very attractive individuals, we both still saw ourselves as the ugly friend that no one wanted to date.

When Kourtney caught wind that I had been seeing other people, he set out on a quest to let me know he had hoes too! He posted pictures of himself with other girls and even flirted with some in front of me. One evening, he intentionally invited me to a gathering with some of his friends, then disappeared in the back room with some random chick. Later he'd call me as if nothing happened and I played along, acting completely unbothered. Sound familiar? I pretended his actions had little to no effect on me because I obviously didn't have an issue attracting men to me. Now keeping them was a different story. But I had removed all feelings from this situation because he was grown and single. Therefore, what he chose to do and with whom he chose to do it with was none of my concern. Additionally, from where I stood, the ladies he had chosen to entertain were no competition.

Usually, I'm not one for games, but when I do decide to play, I rarely play fair. While he paraded numerous insignificant females around me, I, in return, went straight for the jugular. I took the extra petty step of being very flirty with one of his friends. I never let his friend hit, but I made Kourtney believe he did just to get under his skin. It was childish but I didn't care. If he thought I was just going to sit there and let him make me look stupid, he was messing with the wrong one. Anything he would do, I would do better, or worst depending on how you looked at it. We were both adolescents living in grown folks' bodies, doing grown folks' things and making grown folks' mistakes. We were both broken, so there was no way we would have ever worked out anyway.

Our union began to deteriorate. The closer we became, the more evident it was that we couldn't handle what was happening between us. Instead of fully embracing our feelings for one another, we rejected them which caused a multitude of friction and unhealthy displays of affection. One day, I left work early due to food poisoning. I rushed home for what would be an intimate relationship with my toilet. Several trips to the restroom and multiple swigs of stomach-calming medicine later, I passed out in my bedroom with the light shining brightly on my despair. Kourtney had hit me up a few times while I was asleep. After several unreturned calls and texts, he decided to drive past my apartment. The light in my bedroom was still on and I believe Jade had come in to check on me at the exact moment he rode past our apartment. He became very agitated seeing shadows in my bedroom. I woke up the next day to an abundance of disgruntled texts and voicemails. His expiration date was renewed shortly after that incident. Our faux love story had gone on long enough and there was no fairy tale ending in sight.

ALWAYS HAVE AN EXIT STRATEGY

Being promiscuous had its pros and cons. Yes, my reputation was in the garbage, but I had learned how to think and act like men, which was somewhat beneficial. One thing about men is they never over complicate ending a relationship. When they are done, they're done. It's women who usually beg for closure and ask the guy for another chance. Well, this time I was going to take a page from the manipulator handbook and just end all communication. Just like Isaac had stopped calling me when he no longer wanted to date me, I'd deploy the same strategy on Kourtney. As immature as it sounded, I was comfortable with that plan of action. Kourtney, however, was not. He texted, called, DM'd and I could've sworn I seen a carrier pigeon on my stoop one day. They all went unanswered until one day he ran up on me at our local grocery store. I'd originally stopped by the supermarket to shop for items to meal prep for that week, but nothing could've prepped nor prepared me for that conversation. I was nervous. My mouth was dry, and my palms were sweating. What was he going to say? Was he going to curse me out and make a huge scene in the avocado aisle? I didn't know. I tried to walk away but he cornered me and made me face him. I don't remember the whole conversation because my mind was going a mile per minute. He didn't raise his voice because he still cared about me but, he did let me know that he was tired of my bull and wouldn't be putting up with it any longer. Stubbornly, I remained silent, desperately trying to maintain my savage demeanor. Kourtney knew me well enough to know I wasn't going to argue with him, so he took one last look at me, shook his head, and left. Rightfully so. I was sick of myself as well but was unwilling to take the necessary steps to get it together.

SENDING IN YOUR REPRESENTATIVE ALWAYS BACKFIRES

Immediately, I was reminded of the recruiter that I hired to update my resume. The content of my resume was basically the same, but she finessed it in a way to make me look more competitive. Had I been doing the same thing in my situationships? Had I been introducing people to my representative then bamboozling them with my split personalities after they got hooked? I sat down and had a conversation with all three of my personalities and we agreed that therapy was necessary. Instead of getting help, I dug further into my bag of dysfunction and pulled out a plan to get Kourtney back on the team. Several glasses of wine later, I headed upstairs to take a thorough shower in preparation for the night's festivities. Determined to give Kourtney a reason to stay, I also exfoliated my hands and my lips to ensure a soft yet satisfying experience. My dress was sexy enough to entice but also provided easy access. I headed straight to Kourtney's house with every intention of giving him what I thought would make everything go back to normal. Though I didn't allow myself to verbalize my feelings in the grocery store, I planned to physically express myself as soon as I saw him. When I arrived at his doorstep, he didn't immediately answer the way he used to. I stood on the other side full of emotion but lacking the words to express it.

"Let me in." I whispered, but the volume of the television continually increased and drowned out my pleas.

TAKE YOUR L LIKE A G

He didn't even open the door! I was salty but I deserved that type of treatment. It was probably for the best though because our courtship would have led to nothing but trouble. Crushed by the rejection I had just received, I hopped in the Hyundai that I could barely afford and sped out of his parking lot. My car and mind were now going about eight-five miles per hour on highway I-85. It seemed as though Kourtney's sensitivity had now transferred to me as I almost shed a tear. Almost! I forfeited all of my emotions in that moment. Determined to take my L(oss) like a G(angsta), I continued down the highway to a risky location. As I parked my car in front of Q's house, I contemplated driving back home. Q was trouble and I knew it. I had purposely avoided having sex with him because I knew he would ruin me. I'd been able to navigate his playboy ways by refusing sexual encounters, but that night everything would change. I needed to feel wanted. Kourtney's dismissal of me caused my desperation to move into overdrive. As soon as Q open the door, I attacked him. Ripping his clothes off and kissing him because I was determined to feel better. For some reason, he tried to slow me down. I briefly remember him murmuring about needing to tell me something, but I proceeded to seduce him. Whatever he needed to tell me would have to wait until later. I whispered something naughty in his ear then proceed to kiss his neck and unzip his pants. He struggled to continue to tell me his secret as I persisted on distracting him. Finally, he was completely surrounded by my energy and we were both instantly addicted. Q fell asleep immediately after our wonderful encounter. He temporarily made me forget about "what's his name" so I was able to doze off too.

The smell of fried chicken wings and waffles woke me up the next morning. After I gargled with his off-brand mouthwash, I headed downstairs to help with breakfast. We ate and reminisced on last night's festivities. Both blushing a little while giving detailed play-by-plays. I was just about to suggest a second round of pleasure, but I noticed Q's facial expression had changed. He looked like he had swallowed a chicken bone. Maybe he had to pass gas or even take a full poop. Either way I knew that whatever came next would put a halt on round two.

"So, remember last night when I told you that I needed to tell you something?" he said.

My mind was racing. His gun was on the kitchen table. Had he killed someone before I came over? Were the cops going to burst into his apartment with bullet proof vests and uzis. My mind always goes one hundred percent left when anyone says, "I need to tell you something." Those were the words I initially saw in the DM from ol' girl before she revealed to me that Xavier was living double lives. I hated those words with a passion. I took a big gulp.

"Vaguely", I replied. "Why? What's up?"

"Nicki is pregnant", he blurted out.

Q had never been one to beat around the bush. His honesty was the thing I loved and loathed most about him. Nicki, as well as a few others, were a part of his hoe-rotation. Her name always stood out because I remember him telling me that she bought him clothes and gave him money often. Together we would clown her, calling her stupid, desperate and several other demeaning names. Even though I'd participate in laughing at her, I knew the real reason she was willing to financially support this dude. She was hypnotized by "The Legend". His effect on her was the very reason I never wanted to sleep with him in the first place. Now that I had experienced the goods for myself, I couldn't help but understand why she did the things she did. Even though I could relate to her, I still didn't want to share. There lied the dilemma. A range of unhealthy emotions flowed throughout my body as I sat there trying to properly dissect the information that was just provided to me. The pure bliss that we'd experience just a few hours ago was now overshadowed by a sprinkle of saltiness and a dash of future baby mama drama. Those ingredients were sure to yield a flavorless recipe. I wanted no parts of that. He mentioned something about wanting to be the father he never had and how he didn't want to lose me, but his words seemed to float out of his mouth and disappear into thin air. I couldn't concentrate. Being rejected twice in less than twenty-four hours was an extremely humbling experience.

STOP LETTING LONELINESS CHOOSE YOUR LOVER

My self-esteem was on life support. I left Q's house that afternoon feeling completely defeated. The unholy trinity had dismantled right before my eyes. First Isaac pushed me away, and in return I pushed Kourtney away. Now Q's baby mama would be pushing out his jug head seed in a couple of months. Deep down I knew that none of these faux-mances had the potential to last, but I let the fear of being alone convince me otherwise. That always happened when I let loneliness choose my lover. With my lack of confidence guiding all of my decisions, I had become comfortable with believing that receiving the silver medal of love was better than no medal at all. As much as I complained about men and all the drama that comes with them, it was nobody's fault but my own that I ended up in a cycle of situationships. Determined to change the narrative, I began to detox my life of all the toxic habits and people I had previously welcomed. The first thing I did was go on a blocking spree. Blocking people's access to me was my favorite past time, so Kourtney and Q now joined Tobias and Isaac in the abyss of blocked numbers in my phone. Next, I started working out again to rid myself of the excess pounds and stress that had been accumulated during my dating journey. I had successfully gone from looking like a snack to a cheat meal. Who gains relationship weight without being in an actual relationship? Lastly, I decided to start visiting churches again. I hoped that making all those necessary adjustments would put my life back on the right track.

7

TURN TO YOUR NEIGHBOR

"... Love your neighbor as yourself."
-MATTHEW 22: 39 NIV BIBLE

If you've ever attended service at a black church, you've probably heard the preacher utter the infamous words "Turn to your neighbor". Not sure where this phrase originated from, but it seemed as though it was somewhere in the Baptist handbook. It was probably in the hooting and hollering section right after the part where they teach preachers how to breath all hard into the microphone. I grew up in church, so these dramatics were all too familiar. Especially the *turn to your neighbor* concept. It had become a colloquialism for affirming what the pastor had just said. There were times when I hated this part of the service because it seemed like I always turned to a raggedy neighbor. I'd either get Sister Shake Your Hand Off, who insisted on grabbing your hand and violently shaking it to the rhythm of church organ for a holier than thou affect. Or I'd get Brother Bad Breath, who'd involuntarily let me know everything he'd had for breakfast as soon as he opened his mouth. Where was the old peppermint lady when you needed her? Since we're being honest, sometimes I failed at being a good neighbor as well. I'd completely disobey the pastor's instructions and refuse to look at or talk to the person sitting beside me. Although my lady parts had been known to be mighty friendly, the rest of me was shy and anti-social. The fellowship part of the service always made me nervous, but as I grew older, I started to develop an appreciation for it. Especially since I always felt so lonely.

My loneliness heightened as the lovers' holiday approached. Re-member when Jesus knocked over the tables in the temple in the Bible story in Matthew? Well, that's exactly how I felt when bombarded with all the Valentine's Day flowers, candy, and chocolates at my local gro-cery store. Anything pink or red during the weeks leading up to the holiday were in danger of getting destroyed. Since, I was already on the edge, it felt good to go to church and just have the person sitting in my pew smile at me. I needed that positive interaction. When my neighbor looked at me, they didn't see my horrible past or the shame that I was currently carrying in between my legs. Instead, they saw me the way God saw me. I wish I could tap into those God lenses and see myself in that same way. When I looked in the mirror the person starring back at me was dishonorable and defeated.

SKIP NATIONAL SIDE CHICK DAY

Avoiding church had begun to take a toll on me. Not including God in my everyday life led to horrible decisions and even worst conse-quences. Managing to push my pride aside, I finally joined a church in on Sunday, February 15th. Later, I realized that my membership date and National Side Chick Day were one in the same. God had jokes! I didn't find the jokes funny at all, but I did kind of feel like a side chick at my place of worship. It was a mega church with over five thousand members so there were times when I didn't feel seen. Feeling insignificant, I began to backslide. Truthfully, I was still a little hesitate of putting my trust in the God that had previously played me, I wasn't fully ready to submit to be one hundred percent devoted yet.

RELATIONSHIPS SHOULDN'T BE FORCED

When I was younger, I felt like a relationship with God was always forced upon me. My mother made us go to Children's Church, Regular Service, Prayer Meeting, Vacation Bible School, Bible Study and all the other church programs that took up countless hours of the day. She took that "As for me and my house, we will serve the Lord" scripture seriously, so my sister and I had no choice but to attend church all the time. Now that I was an adult, I could move at my own pace. I decided to join the church but would only do the minimal work required to maintain the Christian stamp of approval. My relationship with church mirrored all my other personal relationships. Half in and half out. I hoped that the half of me that was in, wouldn't get hurt, and prayed that God would still bless the other half that was not entirely devoted. This half effort approach to relationships would never work. One hundred percent effort was required. Unfortunately, I didn't have any additional percentages to give. My trust in the Savior was at an all-time low. I was smart enough to know I couldn't run from Him forever, but just dumb enough to think He'd be satisfied with half of me.

Even though I didn't plan to fully pledge my allegiance to the Lord again yet, I still took an all-day discipleship session at my new church home. That was an obligation for new members to fill immediately after joining the church. The session included classes on prayer, faith, giving, etc. There was also a portion solely dedicated to showcasing all the ministries that were available for servanthood. I researched the active list of ministries at my church and the only one that looked worthwhile was the Men's Ministry for obvious sinful reasons. It felt like joining a ministry was a requirement rather than a suggestion. Why do Christians always force Jesus on people? It's my understanding that God's love was supposed to be a gift, but the way church was set up, it always seemed as though something was owed in return. The Baptist barter system had a way of sneaking up at the most inopportune time. People should join ministries because it's in their hearts, not because it's an unwritten rule in the new members' handbook. When I was twelve years old, I decided to give my life to the Lord so I got baptized. Immediately afterward, I remember feeling as though I wasn't saved for real because I refused to go down to the church's basement to try to speak in tongues. Basements frightened me, and I thought speaking in tongues was weird. Every time my mother spoke in tongues, she would accidentally slap me! Or, while doing the hallelujah dance, she'd manage to step on the white patent leather shoes that she forced me to wear. As a pre-teen, I was willing to forgo salvation if that was what it entailed.

Growing up in the church seemed to be a gift and a curse. It was awesome to grow up knowing that some infinite being was always watching over us and meticulously ordering our steps. It was also a little disheartening to feel like that same infinite being was so far away that you could never get close enough to be in His presence. Closeness was a necessity for me. With God being so far away, I didn't feel like that was an option. Therefore, I never rushed to choose Him for myself and never got to fully experience the so-called joy of having a personal relationship with Him. And when I finally did, I was disappointed. He was always my mom's and grandmother's God, and I had the nerve to believe I was a shoo-in for heaven by being related to them. They both had enough Jesus combined that I thought they could secure salvation for the whole family. If I were affiliated with them and fulfilled the requirements on the "Church Girl Checklist," I'd be straight. The pressure of trying to fit in a box that I hadn't chosen for myself and wasn't sure I believed in, became exhausting. In addition, several falsehoods were ingrained in my life from the super Christians in my church.

The Bible in Romans says, "If you declare with your mouth, 'Jesus is Lord,' and believe in your heart that God raised him from the dead, you will be saved." Conversely, my childhood church strongly suggested that you weren't officially saved and weren't getting into heaven unless you could speak in tongues. You had to be a cheerful giver during all one hundred and one offerings collected during every service. You had to cover your head with a prayer scarf or an obnoxious bedazzled church hat before entering the Sanctuary. If you wore pants to church, you would go to hell. And finally, no sex before marriage. There are sixty-six books in the Bible, most of them filled with God's promises of what we can achieve through Him, but it seems that my childhood church specifically focused on what we couldn't do. I successfully made it through the first seventeen years of my life, adhering to most of the mandates listed above. Besides being fake saved because I couldn't speak in tongues, I had managed to squeeze myself into the church girl box prescribed to me. Somewhere during puberty, I slowly began to break free from the Christian cage that I had been put in. Up until then, I did what I was taught. I attended church regularly. I happily placed my dollar bill in the offering receptacle, and strategically placed that ugly laced prayer scarf in my ponytail. The whole no sex before marriage theme was a hard concept to grasp because I was surrounded by several baby showers but not as many weddings to match.

CHURCH GIRLS AREN'T ALWAYS INNOCENT

Since fornication wasn't a foreign concept, I did what I saw instead of what I was taught. I lost my virginity to the neighborhood nerd in the family room of his parents' house. He was hardly the boy next door, and the experience was nothing to write home about, but it did change my life forever. Since I partook in premarital relations, I believed that

I was no longer a part of the kingdom. I had sinned the impartible sin. God was mad at me, and I couldn't speak to Him in tongues to attempt to save my life, so all hope was lost. Those were the types of things that I told myself. I didn't know much about God's grace and mercy, so I associated having sex with being far from God. Fast forward several years later, I still felt the same way.

No matter how hard I tried, I would never be the perfect Christian, and I longed for someone to tell me that it was okay. It would be a long shot because Christians were the most judgmental beings on earth, as well as the most hypocritical. Over the past few years, I sat back and watched many Christians condemn others for the same things they had done. Sex seemed to be the most controversial topic. Many church mothers turned their noses up at pregnant teenagers in the church. All the while, those same mothers with the big ol' church hats were big ol' freaks back in their day. Their lack of acceptance had always been a big turn off. Worldly individuals seemed to be more accepting, and that was why I gravitated toward them. When I wanted to run from God and everything He stood for, I always dabbled in sexual activity. I figured that was the best way to get Him and His Christians to leave me alone.

F-BOYS LOVE THE LORD TOO

Many of my adult behaviors stemmed from childhood. Especially, my view on relationships. I considered myself to be a Believer but tended to bend the rules and not fully adopt all the principles. Consequently, I dated men who had the same outlook. Let's use Tobias as an example. He was in a so-called relationship but did not fully adopt all of the principles of being in one. Apparently, he had a girlfriend the whole time we were messing around, so he let the principle of being faithful fall by the wayside. Additionally, he lacked trustworthiness. I often wondered if she knew he wasn't committed to their relationship, would she have followed through with the marriage. If I were her, I would definitely gave him back to the streets and dropped him off on the side of the road where he belonged. This whole scenario made me think about how quickly we give up on people by not allowing them to apologize for their mistakes and redeem themselves. God is the complete opposite. Time and time again, He forgives us for the stupid things we do. Yet we take advantage of Him and continue to run toward things He's told us to flee from.

God sends little nudges here and there to let us know if we need to change directions. When I met this random guy one day, a strange, overwhelming feeling came over me telling me to run, but I did the exact opposite. It was a holiday weekend, and Atlanta is known to have an event for every occasion. My homegirl and I attended this family friendly event with good music and good food. When we got there, she tried to introduce to me to one of her friends. She had been telling me how good of a guy he was and how it was time for me to settle down. He seemed nice but I couldn't take my eyes off the man next to him. He was a big dude, but his roundness didn't bother me because I knew that meant he'd always have some type of snacks with him. Completely ignoring the man that I was supposed to be getting to know, the other guy and I found a space far away from everyone else. We talked for what seemed like hours. He too had grown up in church, so the conversation started with him telling me how much he loved the Lord. We told each other our favorite scriptures and joked about how our parents forced us to attend every service under the sun. We also talked about sports, food, travel and of course love.

"I don't know what it is about you, but I can really see myself being with you forever. What did you do to me?" He laughed.

This was not the first time I'd had this effect on a man, so I just blushed and continued to bless him with my essence. Somehow, we got on the subject of weddings and began planning ours. I had just met this man a couple hours prior, but we planned to be married in six months. What was I doing? This was completely out of character, but I was hypnotized by his charm and drank his words as if they were glasses of champagne. We were going to be together. Nothing or no one could convince me otherwise.

"I hope I'm not being too forward, but do you want to get out of here and celebrate?"

He wasn't being forward at all in my opinion. I was ready to go home with him as soon as we finalized our wedding plans, but I had to play it off. Not wanting my Jezebel spirit to chase him away, I acted as if I wasn't sure. My friend and I had come to the event together, so I told him that I wanted to make sure she was okay first before leaving. He agreed and I searched for my friend. Immediately upon finding her I asked her what she was about to do. That was code for, I know we came together but we aren't leaving together. Her look of confusion was funny and familiar. This wasn't the first time I had ditched her to go get some action. I basically told her that she needed to find a ride home because she couldn't come with me. I offered to pay for her taxi, but she had real friends at the event that would make sure she got home safely. She told me to be careful, but I didn't heed her warning. I was ready to go and start my new life with this stranger.

He embraced me as soon as I got back to him. He could tell by the look on my face that I was ready to go. He had already taken care of the bill and told me that we could leave as soon as he came back from the restroom. My heart seemed to be dancing to the beat of the church song "Joyful, Joyful". This was what I had been waiting for, a man who knew what he wanted. Me! As I gazed off into the distance, smiling from ear to ear, I saw a young girl approaching from my peripheral.

"Excuse me." She said.

Ignoring her, I continued in my pure bliss. My wedding would be in six months and I had so much to do. Who would design my dress? What venue would we choose? Who would watch all my relative's bad kids while we wed because I definitely planned on having a childless reception? Imagine me planning all this in my head while not even knowing what my new last name would be.

"Excuse me, ma'am." She interrupted.

"What?! What do you want?" I yelled, annoyed that she had called me "ma'am", as if I looked old or something.

"You know my uncle is married, right?"

I wanted to punch his niece in the throat. Not only was she not minding her own business, but she just ruined what could have been my only chance to walk down the aisle. She had probably just saved me from a lifetime of humiliation but something in me still wanted her to go outside and get me a switch, so that I could give her a whooping. True to form, I just got up and left. Accustomed to not expressing my feelings when they get hurt, I stormed out to the venue and headed toward my car. Suddenly, I heard the pitter patter of infidelity following behind me. When he finally caught up to me, he asked why I was going to leave without even saying goodbye. I made it clear that it was the same reason he was going to let me go home with him even though he was married.

"I'm not married, I'm separated!" He said confidently.

If my brain would have allowed me to do what I was thinking, I would have gone to jail. How dare he act as if being separated gave him freedom to plan a life with someone else? Audacity must have been on sale because he had a whole pile in his possession and was giving it out generously. After a few choice words, I flew out of the parking lot leaving that dusty man looking helpless in my rearview mirror.

LEARN WHEN TO KEEP IT MOVING

When I got home, I couldn't wait to tell Jade how I almost made the biggest mistake of my life. She a threw a party that weekend to make me feel better. I didn't have many friends, so I couldn't really contribute to the guest list, so I left that up to Jade. She sent out one tweet and the next thing you know our house was filled with several guests. My heart immediately sank when Kourtney walked in. I had forgot that although I had blocked him from my social media, he still followed Jade. That was the first time I had seen him in months, and he looked tasty. I was surprised that he showed up, though. I thought he despised me, especially after the way our last encounter ended. All the hate must have disappeared because he hugged me tight as soon as he saw me. Energy shot through our bodies as we embraced. We skipped the small talk and went straight to the bar. After numerous mixed drinks and Jell-O shots, Kourtney and I found ourselves in my room. No clothes, no condom, just passion.

"Why haven't you returned any of my calls?"

I didn't answer his question, but he could tell by the confused look on my face that I hadn't received any of his messages. He knew I had blocked him. After several minutes of silence, he just grabbed my phone and unblocked his number. It took him a while to find his number among all the other men that were listed. My blocked list was a valley of dry bones, but I had no desire to revive them. Kourtney wanted to give us another chance, but I knew it was a bad idea. Our situation was defective, and I didn't want to drag Him through all my insecurities again. It was time for our love to die. With a hug and a passionate kiss, I decided to let go forever. The kiss almost convinced me to consider going back to him, but I knew the best thing to do was to stand my ground. Confucius once said, "A man that has committed a mistake and doesn't correct it is committing another mistake," and this mistake was sure to haunt me for the days to come.

The next few weeks were a blur. Kourtney called me a few times as well as sent me a few interesting pictures, but I never responded. Keeping in touch with him would have caused more trouble. Our relationship had no future, and I knew it. That's why I completely freaked out the next month when my period was late. One night of pleasure was potentially about to cause me nine months of turmoil. Taking the pregnancy test was nerve-racking, As I sat on the toilet waiting for the results, I couldn't help but get sick to my stomach. My Hot Girl Summer would potentially turn into Knocked-Up Fall. Oh, if the mothers of the church could see me now. Why did I even put myself in that situation? I could barely take care of myself, let alone another human being.

PRAY ABOUT IT

"Dear Heavenly Father, if you get me out of this one, I promise I'll never have sex again until I'm married. Amen."

My prayer was short, but I had never prayed that hard in my life! My hand was trembling as I reached for the stick to read the results. I paced back and forth, trying to muster up enough courage to check the test. It was negative! Although I felt far from God, I still thanked Him for removing that burden from my life. After thanking God, I became very still and silent. Suddenly the silence turned into a loud, uncontrollable cry. They weren't tears of joy but instead of sadness. Memories of my teenage abortion began to attack me. That was a decision I'd never forget and often regretted. Deep down on the inside, I secretly hoped that I was pregnant so I could have a do-over. That would've been my second chance, and I wasn't going to make the same mistake again. Even though I had my fair share of failed relationships, I honestly had so much love to give, and having a child would've finally guaranteed that someone would love me back. Not only was my belly empty, but so was my life. The Dalai Lama said, "We can never obtain peace in the outer world until we make peace with ourselves."

My life choices caused me to always doubt myself. Depression set in, and I found myself wallowing in guilt. I couldn't find it in my heart to forgive myself for what I had done all those years ago. Forgiveness of self was by far one of the hardest courses of action to take. I drowned my sorrows in a fifth of brown liquor that night. I could've easily crawled into someone's bed, but for the first time in a long time, I felt like sex wasn't the answer. I needed to take a step back to reevaluate my life without distractions. The alcohol briefly numbed my pain, but I still needed to forgive myself. Until I was able to do so, scars of my past would remain very visible.

8

LEAD US NOT INTO COMPARISON

"Comparison is an act of violence against the self."
-IYANLA VANZANT

Later I realized, the men in my life were never of much value to me. They were just a means to an end. My experience with Xavier turned me inside out, leaving me desperate for attention. Attentiveness was what I sought after, and they happily complied. On the contrary, the pregnancy scare awoke a part of me I didn't even know still existed. I didn't want a baby, I wanted what the baby would represent. I entertained a handful of men to prove myself desirable, but later realized I was searching for love. I thought I hated love. Love was heavily associated with heartache, lies, and embarrassment. Who had time for that? Apparently, I did. Previously love had huffed, puffed, and blew my house down, but I wanted it back and was willing to forgo my fears to get it. After my failed pregnancy, I became obsessed with love. It didn't help that it was wedding season. It seemed like everybody and their mama was getting married. All the girls who were hoes in high school had gotten wifed up and were living soccer mom lifestyles. If they made it, certainly I could too. My social media timeline was flooded with corny wedding hashtags such as #ItWasKentToBe, #SpadeForEachOther, and #HappilyEverrettAfter. Jealousy flowed through my veins as I grudgingly double tapped and commented on every wedding related photo. I wanted to be happy for them, but my bitterness wouldn't allow me to do so. They had what I wanted. Or did they? Was the grass greener in matrimony, or was it just artificial turf? I wondered if walking down the aisle to be wed was like walking across the stage for a college degree. When most graduates walk across the stage, they imagine that all their hopes and dreams will be fulfilled once they enter the real world. The sad reality is many graduates enter the workforce in a field that doesn't match what they studied, leaving them feeling inadequate with only a big pile of debt to keep them warm at night. Hopefully, marriage didn't resemble the sham of higher education. While receiving an education is essential, many universities, as well as lenders, have capitalized on people's desire to learn. Sallie Mae and the other mob wives were single-handedly overburdening graduates with debt. Similarly, social media had successfully created a façade of marriage that had all the single ladies craving to post bae-cations with the infamous, "Down to ride till the very end, just me and my boyfriend" caption. We were all getting bamboozled, and I was no exception.

Thirsty for a fiancé, I scrolled through all my social media outlets and sent friend requests to every attractive male I saw. Several guys took the bait, but none of them was a match for what I had in mind. The Bible says, "He who finds a wife, finds a good thing." I guess my future bae sucked at hide-and-go-seek, thus, I had to intervene. After all, I was supposed to be a helpmate, right? Since everyone else was boo'd up, I became heavily motivated to do the same. I even went as low as looking on one of the world's largest professional networks for a potential beau. While stalking the networking site, I noticed a handsome gentleman who worked at a popular entertainment company. There was an opening in his company's accounting department, so I jumped at the opportunity to apply, in hopes that I could jump his bones later. It turned out; he didn't even work there anymore. He dodged the bullet because I probably would've ruined his life. The experience wasn't wholly a loss, though. I landed the position and gained instant access to perks such as tickets to concerts and professional sporting events. They even provided me with a signing bonus, which I used to pay the security deposit on my new apartment. For the first time since I had moved to Atlanta, I felt like a real adult. It was a fantastic feeling to be able to stand on my feet finally. However, it was disheartening to know that I had no one with whom I could share that accomplishment. No matter how much progress I made, unhappiness always seemed to have me in a choke hold.

Thankfully, the demands of my new job left me with little time to wallow in my state of isolation. Two months into my position, I realized I had bitten off more than I could chew. My department needed a full overhaul, and somehow, I volunteered to manage the project. Late nights and early mornings led to mood swings and shots of alcohol. The exhaustion that I felt at the end of each night momentarily kept me out of trouble. My crazy work schedule lessened the chance of me winding up in some random person's bed. I had unintentionally taken a hiatus from my sexual shenanigans without even realizing it.

DON'T SING THE BITTER BRIDESMAID'S BLUES

Trouble seemed to follow me wherever I went, so I suspected it wouldn't be long before I faced foolery. In fact, I was expecting it, especially since my friend CJ's wedding was right around the corner. A group of college friends in a confined space, with alcohol and no real adult supervision, was sure to lead to a ratchet good time. Ready for the much-needed vacation, I happily packed my bag and headed north. The six-hour drive from Atlanta to the wedding's destination gave me plenty of time to reflect on my current situation. I had been avoiding talking to God lately because I had been backsliding. It was just God and I on the open road so I could no longer hide. I had to listen to what He had to say, and it wasn't pretty. He knew that I was irritated with Him because of the lack of courtship in my life. Yet, even through my disappointment, God was still ordering my steps. What started as a crazy quest to find an admirer through social websites, turned into my landing a position that allowed me to become financially independent. God was still looking out for me, so I couldn't understand why He freely offered to be the God of my career, but not the God of my companionship. He always seemed to get me where I needed to be as far as my profession was concerned, but He didn't have that same energy when it came to personal life. It's as if He wanted me to be alone. I thought He said it wasn't right for man to be alone, but apparently, that scripture held true for everyone except me.

A passage in Proverbs says, "Trust in the Lord with all your heart; do not depend on your understanding. Seek His will in all you do, and He will show you which path to take." I felt the Lord telling me to trust Him, but it was tough for me to do so since I had thought He let me down before. I was holding a grudge against God, and it was preventing me from flourishing in many areas of my life. Unsure of how to move past my pain, I remained in the unhealthy cycle of doubt and fear. My GPS instantly interrupted my talk with God, yelling at me to get off at the exit. I proceeded to the route, checked into my hotel, then took a nap to preserve my energy for the time ahead of me. After my nap, I squeezed into my form-fitting attire, poured some poor decisions in my glass then headed to the shuttle for the wedding. The wedding was aboard a beautiful ship. The ceremony was on the top deck, directly beneath Heaven and overlooking the still water. Simply beautiful! CJ's husband cried as she walked down the aisle. They've been together since sophomore year, so everyone else in our graduating class was crying too. It was about time they jumped that darn broom. Everything from the captain themed ceremony decor to the miniature engraved ship party favors were done beautifully. CJ always had a knack for that type of stuff. The music selection was dope too. It was the perfect mixture of old school R&B and the classic hood hits. My college crush should have performed at the wedding, but he made a last-minute cancellation. It was unfortunate because I was so excited to reunite with him and hopefully make some bad decisions that would later yield good stories. Luckily, the eye candy was in abundance, so my crush's absence was hardly noticeable. CJ had strategically placed me at the singles' table. I wasn't sure if she was up to no good or down for the cause, but I was more than willing to participate in the experiment. A young man named Malik sat right next to me. Before his arrival, I had stared at his name tag, hoping he would be attractive. He didn't disappoint me. His skin looked like Reese's peanut butter cups, and he smelled like answered prayers. A tattoo that stated "Faith Over Fear" peeked out at me from his button-up shirt. Out of the corner of my eye, I noticed he kept looking at me and licking his lips.

We managed to engage in a little small talk until it was time to get in the huddle to catch the bouquet. It was the part I least enjoy at weddings—the part where they showcased all the desperate girls that couldn't find or keep a man. Yet, I found myself amongst the pack of wolves waiting for my chance to catch the magical wifey maker. Shortly after winning the invisible, yet implied guarantee of marriage, I found myself in Malik's arms on the dance floor. Our lips were close enough to touch, but I turned away. During our short conversation at the table dedicated to the young and the horny, I learned that he was only a senior in college. There was a significant number of years between us. He was destined to partake in at least ten more years of stupidity where relationships were concerned. Although I was prone to making less than perfect choices, I was used to doing so with guys my own age. Being a cougar didn't interest me at all, so I managed to avoid an unnecessary interaction that night. Plus, I wasn't feeling very sexy after a night full of twerking and sweating. By the time the reception was over, my edges had looked like they needed to touch the hem of Jesus's garment. Exhausted from the night's festivities, I just took a shower, wrapped my hair, and went to bed, alone.

The next day, I felt extremely grateful that CJ opted out of having a bridal party. Not only because it allowed me to relax and take in the gorgeous scenery, but I wasn't emotionally prepared to be a bridesmaid again. Being a bridesmaid was like being the ultimate side chick. Think about it. You get all dressed up to walk down an aisle. You walk toward a man who is ready and willing to commit. The catch is, he's not willing to commit to you. So, there you are, walking toward the idea of something that you gravely crave, yet you're forced to watch from the sidelines. A little while after I moved to Atlanta, I was the Maid of Honor at my baby sister's wedding. Just a few short months after finding out the love of my life was a fraud, I found myself smack dab in the middle of my hopes and dreams, except they had someone's else name on them. No amount of counseling or fermented beverages could successfully remove me from the level of defeat I felt. Those memories of being the jealous Maid of Honor made me even more thankful that CJ had decided against it.

As I drove back to Atlanta, I glanced over at the bouquet that I had caught during CJ's reception and was suddenly overwhelmed with emotion. Superstition tells us the woman who catches the bride's bouquet will be the next to wed. Well, I had caught the bouquet at my sister's wedding and was still very single. Typically, I try to refrain from comparing myself to other women, but I couldn't help feeling that something was wrong with me. My baby sister and I grew up in the same household with the same morals instilled in us. Yet she was four years younger than me, but ages ahead of me where romance and stability were concerned. Similarly, my girl CJ and I went to the same college and took most of the same courses, but somehow, I ended up at the losers', excuse me, the singles' table at her wedding drooling over an adolescent man child. Before I knew it, I had thrown the bouquet out the window. I had a tough time understanding how I had the same foundation as these women but was nowhere close to heading down the path of marriage. Were they prettier than me? More educated? More fun? What was their secret sauce? I loved them both dearly, they were my family, but I'd be lying if I said I wasn't envious of their courtship credentials. They say, enjoy the journey because getting there is half the fun, but in the words of Erykah Badu, "I think I made a wrong turn back there somewhere."

THE GRASS ISN'T ALWAYS GREENER ON THE OTHER SIDE

When I got back to Atlanta, I was an emotional wreck. Happy, glad, jealous, and mad. You name it, I felt it. Jade and I hadn't spent much time together since we were no longer roommates, so I called her to meet me for a girls' night. We went to happy hour at this little lounge in Midtown decorated with bar swings. The see-through top I wore had my mountains peaking to perfection. Jade wore a catsuit that had her yams looking like Sunday dinner. Dressed to impress, we entered the bar and immediately caught everyone's attention. Random guys kept stopping by our section and buying us drinks. The music was going, and the drinks were flowing, which caused all our inhibitions to slowly become nonexistent. Jade and I began to dance suggestively on one another, which attracted a situation neither of us expected. Two females walked up to us and started buying us shots. We never turned down free drinks, plus they were kind of cute, so we welcomed their presence. I remember stumbling to the restroom and throwing up all the free liquor that I had recently earned. After I thoroughly rinsed my mouth out and freshened my breath with pieces of gum, I returned to our section. When I returned, our two new friends offered to take us to the strip club. I hadn't visited any of the strip clubs since I had relocated to Georgia, but that night would be the night of many firsts. I got in the passenger seat of my new friend's Lexus while Jade rolled with the other girl. I didn't remember much from that night because I blacked out several times. The only thing I did remember was kissing the girl at a red light then pulling into some random underground parking space to finish what we had started. I'm unsure of all that transpired once we were in the parking garage, but I didn't have on any panties, which provided easy access for my bisexual cherry to popped.

The next morning, I woke up in Jade's bathtub, covered by a sea of toilet paper. Jade was on the floor next to the toilet wrapped in the shower curtain. The full details of that night will forever be a mystery. Simple tasks like walking and talking were a struggle that morning, so memories were the least of our worries. I prayed to God that we weren't stupid enough to drive ourselves home that night. I peeked out the blinds but was unable to locate my car. Searching for clues in my phone, I stumbled upon a text from a random 404 area code number that read.

"Hey babe, this is Theory. Call me when you can function properly lol."

It all came back to me. She had helped us get home safely. I sang her praises and told her that I owed her big time. We texted back and forth every day after that night. We even linked up to watch some movies, but you know how all my movie nights go. It was kind of weird because I was on the verge of being in my first real relationship in over four years, but this time I would be in a relationship with a female. Although that was my first consensual bisexual experience, I'd be lying if I said I hadn't always been curious.

When I was a kid, a family friend molested me. We were a few years apart in age, and I had always considered us as a family until she took advantage of me. I believe my curiosity stemmed from that experience. I was too young to know what was going on, but as I grew older, there was always something in the back of my mind encouraging me to experiment. Before now, I never told anyone about my molestation except Xavier. I had no hard feelings against the young lady because I don't believe she fully understood what she was doing either. Her mom was a crackhead and had dope boys running in and out of their house all the time. Her mother would do anything for another hit, so I'm sure she probably entertained females for drugs, and that's where her daughter picked up on it.

Nonetheless, I was now ready to experiment with my feelings toward the same sex, but there was an issue preventing us from doing so. My new girlfriend had a boyfriend. I couldn't win. Even when I switched teams, I was still a side chick. Eventually, Theory and I parted ways. She was beautiful but wanted me to do too much for her. Somehow, she figured I would be the guy in the relationship and was, therefore, responsible for courting her. Things would never work out with us because I refused to jump through hoops for intimacy that had to be strapped on. I wanted the type of love that could not be easily detached. Unfortunately, she couldn't provide that for me so I had to let her go.

9

FREE WILL AIN'T CHEAP

"The reason why it's so important for you to understand the power of
even so-called casual sex is because there's no condom for your heart.
You might be able to protect your physical body against things that
can be transmitted sexually, but what about the things
that are transmitted spiritually?"
-MICHAEL TODD, RELATIONSHIP GOALS

My experience with Theory made me a little more sympathetic toward Xavier. Maybe he had a similar experience of being molested as a child, and that's why he experimented with guys. Xavier knew my innocence was tampered with at a tender age and how it led to my interest in girl on girl pornography. He knew everything regarding my curiosity about the same sex, so I couldn't understand why he didn't open up to me about the similar battle he was experiencing. He shouldn't have left me in the dark like that. I told him my most embarrassing and unflattering secrets, and he chose to just listen instead of empathizing. It wasn't fair. It was downright rude! I gave him my truth, and all I ever wanted in return was for him to reciprocate. Now more than ever, I was determined to receive the mutual love and respect that only a spouse could provide. Initially, when I found out about Xavier's extracurricular activities, I purposely had sex to make God mad. That was stupid because I was only hurting myself. This time, I would handle things differently in hopes of getting different results. Celibacy had to be the answer. I wanted a husband and was sure abstaining from sex would be the way to get him. The longest I had ever gone without having sex was only a couple of months, so I figured I needed to find a husband soon to prevent an unnecessary drought. If I was going to be celibate, I had to do it cold turkey, ridding my life entirely from miscellaneous men to be successful. There was only one problem, and his name was Malik.

PUT PEOPLE ON YOUR PRACTICE SQUAD

Malik had successfully made a pallet in my DMs ever since we parted ways at my friend CJ's wedding. Slowly but surely, I was inching toward the cougar status. There was about a decade between us. He was probably still in diapers when "Cash Money took over for the 99 and the 2000." Still, there was something about that him continued to intrigue me. He didn't party much, which seemed to be rare for a soon to be a professional athlete. He had been drafted to play for one of the professional sports teams and would be headed to Atlanta for preseason soon. We started with harmless flirting, sending each other risky videos via social media messages that would immediately disappear seconds after being opened. After a couple of weeks of talking, he left tickets for me at Will Call to come to watch him play. He was talented. I enjoyed watching him sweat and often fantasized about us running our plays. However, I promised myself this time would be different, so I tried to stick to the plan. Malik often suggested that we should link up. I held him off for as long as I could until one day, he sent me a video of himself wrapped a towel after he had just gotten out of the shower. The towel was low enough to please, but just high enough to keep me guessing. That did it! We immediately made plans to see each other. He showed up wearing a wife-beater, grey sweatpants, white socks, and Nike slides. With his athletic build, tattoos and sexy lips, I was sure he was out here breaking hearts left and right. He did his best to convince me that he was different, informing me that he was a preacher's kid and therefore was a man of God. All that God-talk went out the window when it came to his sexual appetite though. After he scarfed down the dinner that I had prepared for him, I was next on the menu. He propped me up on the kitchen counter and began kissing me intently. Wrapping my legs around him, he picked me up and threw me on the bed. I've always been a little thick, so I was impressed and significantly turned on by the fact that he could carry me. Things became oddly unsatisfying when he hopped on top me. From the towel picture that he sent; I was sure that he would provide a most joyous experience. However, after several minutes of kissing and groping, his soldier still wasn't standing at attention. He didn't seem up for the challenge, and I didn't want to break my celibacy for someone who couldn't cross the finish line. Maybe I wasn't his type. Whatever the case may have been, I pulled away and suggested that he leave. Malik didn't give up easily. With one hand, he unhooked my bra while using the other to remove my leggings. Removing my pants only revealed that my body parts were ready, and his still weren't. The harder he tried without positive results, the more adamant I became about him leaving. He did so grudgingly.

The videos and text messages were far and few in between after I rejected him. He kicked me off his Will Call ticket list as well. Luckily, I worked for an entertainment company and would often secure sports tickets of my own. Upon my arrival at one of his games, I noticed a woman wearing a replica of his jersey with the letters Mrs. and his last name embroidered on the back. Later, I found out that she was his girlfriend in college and had recently moved to Atlanta to be with him. So much for him not being like the rest. I walked away from that situation with some dignity, which was rare. Normally, I'm angry when a situation ends because I would've given away my goodies for free and had nothing to show for it. This time, since I had stayed faithful to abstaining, I walked away with the confidence of knowing that I had finally won. Malik was nothing more than a passing amusement, and I was super proud of myself that I hadn't let him get the best of me.

The absence of unnecessary men made life quite enjoyable. My confidence began to increase, as well as my church attendance. One Sunday, my pastor announced that the church would be participating in a corporate Daniel's Fast. I wanted to be closer to God, so I decided to join. Immediately upon my completion of the fast, I received a raise at my job. Things were finally starting to look up for me. The only thing missing was a husband, but I was sure he was on his way because I had successfully gone seven months without sex. God saw my progress and was planning to bless me indeed. I had been refraining from my regular sexcapades in hopes that the closing of my legs would force me to open my heart. As the enemy saw me making positive strides in my life, he began to throw everything he could my way. The little things like car troubles and unexpected bills no longer phased me. I had money now so I could handle those types of expenses, but the death in my family truly took a toll on me. Typically, I'd pursue penetration as a means of therapy, but this time, I decided to adopt healthier coping mechanisms. I had been trying to stop the dangerous cycle of self-medicating with sex and alcohol. I realized that happiness was not found in an empty box of condoms, nor at the bottom of a liquor bottle. The best way to deal with that type of stress was to be around family, so I decided to buy a plane ticket to visit home. Unfortunately, I accidentally transposed the departing cities during the booking process, which made my ticket invalid and was in danger of not being able to board my flight.

CO-PARENTING CAN COME WITH CONTROVERSY

Luckily, I remembered that Q had a friend that worked for the airline where I had purchased my ticket. Although we hadn't spoken since he told me Nicki was pregnant, he once said to me that he would always have my back. I wanted to give him a chance to prove to me that his words were true, so I unblocked him then gave him a call. He was excited to hear from me, but I had no time for small talk. After hearing about my dilemma, he had his friend correct my ticket, waive all the fees, and upgrade me to first-class. His actions served as a peace offering and opened the door for regular conversation. After a few very intentional discussions, we concluded that we were meant to be, but the timing was always off. When he wanted to be with me, I was caught up in Isaac's web of deception. And when I wanted him, he had a baby on the way. His child was only a few months old now, but he assured me that he and his baby mama were strictly co-parenting. Q told me he was ready for something real, and with me. Could this be true? Someone wanted me, all of me, not just the kinky parts. This unfamiliar yet exhilarating feeling caused things to escalate quickly between us. My celibacy journey had been going very well up until the moment Q and I decided to be in a committed relationship. As soon as I got back in town, I invited him over to make things official. We were now a couple, and I wanted to do a couple of things to him. Breaking my celibacy was wrong, especially since I had promised God that I wouldn't have sex until I was married. However, God had given us free will and time after time, I used that excuse to do something stupid. This time was no different. I proceeded with my broken promise and disobedience to the Lord, convincing myself that it was okay because Q would eventually become my husband one day. One look led to hours of fornication. All my pent-up energy was finally released.

We spent a lot of time together just enjoying each other's company. It felt good to have a significant other finally, but things began to feel less significant as the days went by. We never went out. We spent the majority of our time in my apartment. At first, I thought it was just because he enjoyed my sweet spot so much. He drove over an hour to see me multiple times per week. That good lovin' had to be the reasons he kept coming back for more. Cocky and naïve, I continued down the path that would eventually lead nowhere. Although Q came to see me often, he'd never spend the night. He'd always give me an excuse about how I lived so far, and he had to be at work early in the morning. Also, when I called him, he would always have to call me back or seemed like he had to change locations before speaking with me. My intuition was telling me that there may have been another girl involved, but I desperately wanted to trust him. Once again, I tried to ignore the signs, but this time I chose to share my concerns with one of the girls in my inner circle. My friend hated to see me distressed, so she used her investigative skills to do some research. The results were in, and they were unfavorable. She sent me several screenshots that showed evidence that Q was living with his baby mama. She had bought a house, and he and his daughter were living there with her as a family. The internet never sleeps and will always remain undefeated.

The screenshot evidence was sent to Q within a matter of seconds. There was no need for me to add any commentary. The pictures spoke loudly enough for themselves. He called immediately, trying to explain himself. He said Nicki had given him an ultimatum. Either they become a live-in couple, or she'd forbid him from seeing his daughter and force him to pay child support. Q said he didn't have a choice. His uncle had kicked him out since he had caught him selling drugs in his basement. He didn't have a place to live and didn't want to spend a life without his daughter, so he agreed to her demands. His sad story did not impress me, especially since it was the first time, I had heard anything about it. We had been together for about a month and a half, and not once did he mention his situation. He specifically told me that he and Nicki were co-parenting, and that was it. He was a liar, and I had no room for any of that. Infidelity seemed to be the new black, and our relationship was on-trend. Things ended just as fast as they had started with Q. The merry-go-round that I called my life had taken me for another spin.

CHECK YOUR SIGNIFICANT OTHER, NOT THEIR LOVER

Q wasted so much of my time. Not only had I broken my celibacy, but now I had also acquired a brand of baby mama drama that could possibly end with a restraining order or a physical altercation. Nicki hated me. She completely skipped over the part where she was supposed to curse Q out for lying and being unfaithful. Instead, she attacked me. One night she got a hold of Q's phone and called me fourteen times. I had been ignoring his calls ever since I found out he'd been playing house with her. Originally, I thought the back to back phone calls were from Q trying to apologize. When I finally answered, I was surprised to hear Nicki's voice on the other line. I immediately went to my home bar to take a shot because I knew I had an interesting call ahead of me. Q had saved my number in his phone as Sweet Spot, so that was our first topic of discussion. She had a pretty good idea as to how I had achieved my nickname, but she demanded to know my real name. I could have been petty and told her that her man knew my name very well, but I refrained. Her tone was unwelcoming, and I didn't take kindly to her, trying to check me. She called me every vulgar name in the book and made up some new ones just in case the originals didn't fully offend me. Our conversation was unproductive and very unnecessary. I had no intention of being a stepmom or sharing a man, so I just said, "You can have him sis" and hung up. She called back several times that night, so I blocked Q's number again and went on about my business. I thought that would be the last time I would hear from her, but I was wrong.

Things were quiet for a while until I walked outside to my car one day and found all four of my tires were flat. Once again, Nicki had hacked into Q's phone and saw my address in his recent trips history. This chick had a vendetta against me, and now it was mutual. If she would've stuck around, I would've happily kicked her teeth in. She had disappeared and it wasn't like I could hop in my car to go hunt her down. As unfortunate as this situation was, it reminded me of when my ex from graduate school was spending too much time with one of his lab partners. Instead of dealing with my significant other, I wanted to fight the girl. That was stupid because she wasn't the problem. He was. Why do we always go after that person who we are not in the relationship with? Yes, the side piece sucks if they knew the person they were dealing with was involved with someone else, but they never made a commitment to be faithful to you. Your lover did though, so they should be on the receiving end of your attitude. It was his or her responsibly to uphold the duties of the relationship. If they fail, give them a chance to redeem themselves or give them the boot. Nowadays, if you beat someone up, you can go to jail or worse, they can pull a gun on you. I wasn't about that life, so I chose to tap into the spirit of un-botheredness. I refrained from retaliating against Nicki. She was stuck with Q, and that was punishment enough.

10

REVELATION

"Sometimes we're looking for love, but we're not ready for it emotionally. There's still some work we need to do on ourselves, some personal heavy lifting that demands focus and concentration and sacrifice for a while longer."
– DEVON FRANKLIN & MEAGAN GOOD, THE WAIT

Being single must only be fun when you're a slut! After my relationship with Q backfired, the idea of dating became less amusing. Especially since fornicating was off the table this time. Immediately after dealing with Q and his psycho baby mama, I decided to jump back on the celibacy horse. Figured I owed it to myself to give it another try. The first year was extremely uncomfortable, gut-wrenching even. Q had awakened my sexual taste buds, so an entire year without any intimate male interactions seemed like cruel and unusual punishment. I deactivated my social media accounts and stayed to myself for a while. If I were to be successful at this whole no sex thing, I had to eliminate all possible distractions.

The slightest form of flattery would be sure to make me revert to my old ways. I longed for affection but knew that letting my flesh win would lead to my ultimate demise. During my season of hiding, I began to research how to succeed in relationships. "The Wait" by Devon Franklin and Meagan Good and "The Five Love Languages" by Gary Chapman were amongst my reading material. Pastor Michael Todd, from Transformation Church in Tulsa, Oklahoma, released an eight-part YouTube series entitled "Relationship Goals," which also laid a solid foundation for my research. The reading material and YouTube series were helpful, but I wanted a hands-on experience. Convinced that my newly found lifestyle would yield a relationship soon, I began to reactivate my accounts and slowly emerge back on the social scene.

I had given up my promiscuous ways and was now ready for my reward. I was ready to begin actively dating again, but my heart wasn't. My trust issues were standing in the way of my full recovery. During my quest to get back in the swing of things, I met a few guys but had stopped saving their numbers on my phone. Previously, I had the tendency of unblocking people after removing them from my life, so I had to come up with a new strategy. Now, they had to prove themselves to me before securing a spot in my contact list. When I first met a guy, I didn't know his intentions and was unsure of what significance he would have in my life. Therefore, I did not give him a position that he did not deserve. If things went wrong, all I needed to do was erase the text message thread, and suddenly he would disappear as if he never existed. And when he tried to sneak back into my life like nothing happened, I could honestly hit him with the "who dis" text, because I genuinely had no record of him in my phone. It gave me so much joy to unaffectedly detach myself from these random individuals. My sister hated this habit that I had developed. She also said I gave up on people too easily because I'd leave as soon as they made one suspect move. She believed that by not saving people's numbers, I was speaking defeat into existence. My sister felt that I was subconsciously saying the person didn't deserve to be in my life, and that was why they all ended up leaving. I could understand her point of view, but I had become accustomed to the defense mechanisms. Being able to let the guys know that they were never really that important to me was empowering, but my sense of empowerment would quickly fade upon entering my next situationship.

Time flew by, and it was time to celebrate my birthday. My girls and I went to Jamaica in hopes of finding a vacation bae; however, our travel agent booked us at what seemed like a retirement home resort. A bunch of older people surrounded my friends and me. We arrived at the pool in thong bikinis, ready for fun. Meanwhile, the elderly people were doing water aerobics while listening to the music that was playing when the Titanic ship sank. It wasn't the type of environment that encouraged romance or enjoyment of any kind, but I still tried to make the best out of it. My suitcase was filled with enticing attire, and I paraded around my social media timeline as bait. If the guys couldn't come to me, I'd go to them, electronically. Shortly after showcasing myself in my swimsuits, several men were whispering sweet nothings in my DMs. Among them was the guy that I had been crushing on since college. We were originally supposed to reconnect at CJ's wedding, but he made a last- minute adjustment to his schedule, and our plans fell through. It was probably for the best, though, because I knew he could throw me off my game.

"Ayyyeeee, it's my wife's birthday! Happy B-Day bae".

His DM also had several heart eye emojis, but the word "wife" was what significantly grabbed my attention. That word was my kryptonite, especially since I was now in my thirties. For some reason, society had negatively stamped unmarried women over the age of thirty as old maids. Embarrassed and insecure that I had yet to meet society's standards, I'd often allowed myself to rush toward love even if red flags were present. The slightest hint of marriage threw all my common sense out of the window. He hadn't contacted me in over a year. That should've let me know that I was very low on his list of priorities. I should have also been leery that he backed out on performing at my friend's wedding without proper notice. That situation didn't speak highly of his character, but I chose to have temporary amnesia and ignore the warning signs. His DM indicated that he saw me as his wife, and I was willing to do anything to turn his words into reality. His sexy curly hair and salt and pepper beard distracted me as well, so we immediately exchanged numbers and kept in contact while I was on my birthday trip. I wouldn't have saved his number in my phone, but I wanted to heed my sister's advice. She was married and I wasn't. It was best that I followed the blueprint she'd left for me. I saved his number in my phone as *Husbae,* merging husband and bae in the hopes that it would be a self-fulfilling prophecy.

Conversing with him throughout the day became a part of my daily routine once I returned to Atlanta. We spent several hours on the phone, revealing the details of the crush we had on one another for the past several years. We managed to dance around the idea of being together throughout our undergraduate career. Husbae told me that he had always felt rejected by me. He claimed he tried to approach me several times, but I refused to give him a chance. Honestly, I always thought he was a player. He was an entertainer, and his frequent performances caused him to be very popular. His lifestyle yielded a bunch of groupies, and I had no desire to be a part of his following. If we were going to be together, I needed to be number one, not one of many. Thus, I ignored his conquests after me because I never thought he was serious. I feared he was unable to be in a committed relationship, so I refrained from even opening that door. The more we talked, the more I felt a growing bond with him. We had the same views on religion, family, and money. We finish each other's sentences. Everything seemed effortless until feelings got involved.

DON'T INVITE YOUR EX INTO YOUR NEXT RELATIONSHIP

During one of our daily conversations, I strategically asked him, "If you had to describe your love life using a song, what would that song be?" I was falling for him but didn't dare to come right out and say it, so I tried to finesse the conversation to see if he felt the same way. I was hoping he'd choose Beyoncé's, "Crazy in Love" or Drake's, "Best I Ever Had." "You got me sprung, and I don't care who sees" or "Baby you're my everything, you're all I ever wanted.", were the verses that I wanted to come to his mind when he thought of me. Or, since he was an artist, I expected him to write me an original love song that would showcase his feelings for me. After a long pause, he shared that the song he most identified with was "Heartbreaker" by Tank. I had never heard the song before, but judging from the title, I knew he had a wall up that I was now responsible for breaking down. I had to know what I was up against, so I listened to the song intently. The lyrics were as follows:

> "Baby girl, tell me how again I'm supposed to trust you now
>   After everything you admitted to me
>   And I'm sitting here tryin' to find a way to forget somehow
>   'Cause I'm feeling like you cut me too deep
>   Girl, I blame myself 'cause I told you lay it on the line
>   Never thought that you would lay it that way
>   Never thought you had so much to say
>   Never thought that I'd see the day
>   Where we almost cross the line between love and hate
> Are you sure you told me everything?
>   Even though it hurts,
>   I'm tryin' to take it like a man, and halfway understand
>   Being hurt wasn't part of the plan"

That was only the first stanza of the song. My heart bled for him as I listened to the rest of the song, thoroughly examining the lyrics. After an intense conversation, I realized the song accurately depicted a situation from his past. He was a victim of what we Christian's like to call Church Hurt. His ex-girlfriend, along with someone from his former church had took advantage of him, which resulted in several roadblocks to his heart.

Many of us falsely believe that when we are doing work in the Kingdom, we will be shielded from all harm. Conversely, we receive more persecution for being in the will of God than non-believers. Husbae's first and only love had stolen both his heart and his money and later ran off to be with one of the younger deacons. She manipulated him into believing that he was a bad person because he didn't attend church regularly and was heavily involved in secular music. He was the lead singer of his R&B group, but he was willing to give that all up for her. And he did. He was going to church regularly and giving money to her deacon boyfriend in hopes that he could help pray all his sins away. Later he found that it was all a scam, and his relationships hadn't been the same since then. His trust issues were more profound than mine. I didn't think that was humanly possible, but it was. Now I was charged with breaking down the walls that we had both put up and then using those bricks to build a solid foundation for us. That wouldn't be an easy task.

WHEN SOMEONE GHOSTS YOU, DON'T TRY TO RESURRECT THEM

Husbae got ghost for about two weeks after he revealed his broken heart to me. I tried to be understanding because I knew it took a lot out of him to open up about his heartache. It still didn't make me feel good to be left alone. I wanted to talk to him to let him know that I had his back no matter what. It's hard to let someone know how much you care when they don't return your phone calls. Two weeks with no conversation turned my sympathy into rage. Her and I were not the same, yet he was making me pay for her mistakes. I was having a hard time coping with Husbae's silence, so, fortunately, my friend's game night helped me to get my mind off him. Even though I still had him on my mind, I managed to pick up a stray by the end of the game night.

One of my friend's guests had been flirting with me all night, so I allowed him to take me out. While the new guy and I were at dinner, a familiar yet non-frequent name popped up on my caller ID. I excused myself from the dinner table and rushed to the restroom to answer. Husbae just picked up where we left off as if nothing happened. That was the first sign of his bipolar tendencies. I couldn't understand how he went from all that "wife" talk, to not speaking to me for weeks. I was not okay with it but dared not start an argument, especially since I was so glad that we were back together.

While on the phone with him, I just left the restaurant without even saying goodbye to my date. I needed the new guy to be so mad at me that he would never contact me again. And I couldn't tell Husbae that I was on a date. He already didn't trust me because of his ex's mistakes. I couldn't have him not trust me because of mine as well. The whole situation was shady, but I had to do what I had to do to protect our love. We needed to connect on a deeper level, so I decided to invite him into my past. I told him about how Xavier had taken my heart, stomped on it, and used the broken pieces to make dangling earrings. The purpose of telling him about Xavier was to ensure him I would never intentionally cause him pain because I, too, had been hurt before. He needed to know that we were in this together.

MAMA'S BOYS ONLY HAVE ROOM FOR ONE WOMAN IN THEIR LIFE

Each day we became closer. The more we shared, the more in sync we became. Husbae mentioned he was planning to move to Georgia at the end of the year. He felt there was more opportunity in Atlanta to advance his singing career. My heart filled with joy as we started the virtual house-hunting process. He was willing to give up everything he had built in his hometown to move and rebuild something special with me. The end of the year couldn't come quickly enough. I couldn't wait to reunite with him. Things moved quickly, and Husbae introduced me to his mother via video chat. His mother was a sweet lady. She spoke highly of her son, but I left the conversation feeling as though he might be a bit of a mama's boy. She appeared to be fond of me, but I never got the chance to confirm because he became unreachable again. Maybe she didn't feel like I was worthy of being with her son and encouraged him to stop talking to me. Or perhaps I was the first woman he had introduced to his mother since his ex-girlfriend, and that frightened him. Either way, the uncertainty was aggravating me. My anxiety was through the roof. I chose not to gravitate toward another man this time because I knew he would be back. A couple of days passed by and he was still a no call, no show. Worry tried to attack my spirit, but my faith in us sustained me. When he finally returned to me, I had questions. Although I felt strongly about us, I needed to know that he felt the same way about me. If we weren't an item, I'd pick up my pride and let him be. However, if we were indeed a "we," I desperately needed to know why he continuously chose to do life without me.

BELIEVE IN THEIR ACTIONS, NOT THEIR VOCABULARY

When I asked him what we were, he replied, "God sent you to me. You know exactly who you are to me".

That statement told me absolutely nothing, but at that moment, I felt like it was everything. Husbae's used car salesman charade worked on me like a charm. I piled the inconsistency and false hopes of marriage into the mythical luxury hooptie he sold me and rode happily off into the sunset. In my eyes, his words were gold, and I made myself believe him no matter the price. Lacking wisdom, I continued to have faith in our fabricated fairy tale. Our situationship was defective. No matter how hard I tried, it never seemed to function correctly. When things were good, they were perfect. When communication was consistent, we learned so many new things about each other. It was amazing how much we had in common.

Conversely, we had several differences that made things exciting but troublesome at times. For example, discussions about our zodiac signs caused us major controversy. I've always been a spiritual person that believed in the power of visualization and speaking things into existence, but I had never been one to believe in horoscopes. I knew I was a Taurus, but that was about it. He was a Scorpio, and apparently, my sign was the exact opposite of his. He read me the characteristics of his sign, and I remembered feeling very uneasy. There weren't a lot of good traits that were mentioned, yet he seemed proud of them. According to his findings, we would only be fifty percent compatible in the commitment category. Since both our signs were rumored to be extremely stubborn, our compatibility horoscope suggested we'd often have a hard time finding middle ground. Him telling me this didn't seem like a coincidence. I felt as though he was trying to foreshadow our relationship. I'd often use this tactic as well when I was getting ready to exit a complicated situation. I would let my unsuspecting lover know the less flattering things about my personality in hopes that they would just leave. Instead of being an adult and breaking up with them face-to-face, I'd make them aware of my imperfections and encourage them to retreat.

Although our zodiac signs revealed that we would have relationship issues, we passed the sexual compatibility test victoriously. We were hundreds of miles away from one another, so he'd often suggest we satisfy the physical needs in an alternative way. He headed to his studio to play me one of his latest songs. His voice flowed through the phone and caressed every part of my body. When he sang to me, I was putty in his hands. Hanging on to his every word, we decided to take our conversation to FaceTime. He propped his phone up on one of his musical instruments. He needed his hands to be free for what he planned to do next. A little hesitant at first, I just bit my lip and enjoyed the show. Unable to contain my arousal, I quickly became an active participant. Phone sex did not count as a real sex to me, so I was content in knowing that my celibacy was still intact. However, throughout our relationship, I began to feel a little convicted when phone sex became more frequent than regular phone calls.

MAKE THEM GIVE YOU A TITLE OR MAKE YOURSELF UNAVAILABLE

After I declined an invitation for yet another sexual video chat, Husbae dusted off his magical wand and pulled another disappearing act. This time he was only unavailable for two or three days, but it was still two or three days too long. I was done! No longer did I have time to try to piece together that deteriorating relationship. My feelings for him were deep, but to survive, I needed to let them go. His excuses were repetitive and no longer enough. He always blamed his absence on his career, and when that didn't work, he began to blame me. He claimed that I was the one that was ghosting him. He falsely accused me of not calling and texting him often and claimed he was just matching my energy. I sent screenshots of my call log and text history as proof. I had reached out to him several times during his sabbatical to no avail. Instead of admitting that he was wrong, he told me that I was childish and incapable of having an adult conversation. According to him, adults should converse professionally, instead of being petty and sending screenshots. He was certified crazy!

Somehow my proof of his lack of participation in our fauxmance transformed into my level of pettiness and inability to discuss issues properly. I had several screenshots in the arsenal that could further prove my point, but I deemed them unnecessary to send. The situationship was over, so there was no need to prolong the inevitable. I asked him to stop calling me, but he wouldn't listen. I heard from him more after we had broken up than when we were together. Eventually, I added him to the infamous blocked list with the rest of the time-wasters. He needed to know that he couldn't pick me up and drop me off whenever he felt like it. If he wanted me, his actions needed to be aligned. A couple of weeks after I blocked him, I began to miss him. I had too much pride to remove him from my blocked phone list, so I turned to social media to get his attention. Shortly after posting my picture, his name, and more heart eye emojis popped up in my DMs again. I hated the heart eye emoji now and wanted it to die a slow, agonizing death. I felt like it was taunting me. Those were the same emojis Husbae used when he made the "wife" comment. It was also the same emoji he'd use when he'd return from his frequent leaves of absence. Now he chose to use the emoji to communicate with me instead of apologizing and sealing his apology with changed behavior. His DM was left unanswered. I hoped my silence would convey that I was a once in a lifetime opportunity. If he wanted to be with me, he had to be willing to work for it. Over the next several months, he continued to DM me, but none of his words offered reassurance of our recovery.

Often, I wouldn't respond because I wanted him to know how it felt to want to speak with someone and not be able to reach them. After several unanswered messages, he stated that he felt as though I no longer cared. His assumptions were correct. I guess I had left all my cares in the same place he left my relationship title. He had never officially made it clear if we were in a committed relationship, but a four-letter word gave me a blind allegiance to him. I desperately wanted to be a wife, so I completely ignored all the consistent inconsistencies in our communication. I hoped that my patience would inspire a significant change in him, which would lead to a fruitful relationship. Two willing participants were needed for that to happen, and neither of us was up for the task. Eventually, the messages ceased, and so did my expectations of him and anything he had to offer. He used to make me feel like a million bucks, but when it was all said and done, I felt like a bag of unrolled pennies. It was time for Husbae and I to get a divorce.

Abstaining from my ex-Husbae was difficult but painfully necessary. One phone call from Husbae would've made me stupid all over again, so I was relieved I had blocked his access to me. Although I knew we'd be better apart, there was still a part of me that wondered if we could ever get that old thing back. I had plans to visit the Midwest soon to welcome my nephew into the world and pondered on having him meet up with me while I was in town. Then it dawned on me that if he didn't come to visit while we were slightly together, he wouldn't come to see me when we weren't. The distance hurt us, especially since physical touch was both of our love languages. Maybe if he could've followed through with his plans to move to Atlanta, things would have turned out differently.

The foolish parts of me wanted to believe this to be true, but the little bit of saneness I had left, encouraged me to seek spiritual guidance. Except for my false pregnancy debacle, I had never prayed that hard in my life. Desperate for answers, I cried out to God, asking Him for a sign. Here's the thing that sometimes ticked me off about God. When I asked for little things, like a small waistline, He'd laugh in my face, while allowing my gut to sit on my lap. But oh no, when I asked Him about this guy, he bombarded me with several scenarios to encourage my exit. I swear it was like as soon as I uttered the last word of my prayer, toxic situations began to flood my memory. The rumors of him messing around with a married woman while we were in college moved to the forefront of my brain. If that weren't enough to deter me, I also remembered that he had smashed one of my good friends back in the day. Now, it was a one- night stand, and both parties involved assured me that it meant nothing. However, I was still close with this friend, so that made the situation extremely awkward for me. All signs were pointing toward the exit. These situations didn't speak very well on his behalf, but I, too, had a very dark past and felt it was unfair for me to judge him for his wrong decision. Both of those scenarios had happened before we chose to deal with each other, so I tried to forgive his past mistakes in hopes that we could secure a promising future. God was sure to remind me that even though those unpleasant moments happened in the past, our current situation was full of buffoonery as well. I was quickly reminded of how unwanted I felt when he would leave for days and sometimes weeks. His abandonment didn't stop there. During our very last conversation, I told him that I loved him. My statement was misguided, but it was sincere. The proper response would've been "I love you too" or something similar. Instead, he chose to tell me that I was too controlling and needed to stop rushing things. If that wasn't the slap in my face begging me to move on, I don't know what was. My loneliness heightened my vulnerability. Thankfully, grace and mercy were there acting as sidekicks preventing me from further ruining my life. Suddenly, I had a revelation that God had been with me the entire time those negative situations were flipping my life upside down. Just as Mary had an encounter with Jesus in John 20 but didn't realize it was Him, I realized the Lord had been fully invested in all my relationships, strategically rerouting me away from those He hadn't chosen for me. While I was in Atlanta perverting my purpose, God was using all my missteps to show me who He was and molding me into who He wanted me to be.

11

GENESIS

"If at first you don't succeed, then dust yourself off and try again."
-AALIYAH

R.I.P to the union between Husbae and I. There was no need for a moment of silence. The unanswered calls and texts throughout our relationship contained enough silence to last a lifetime. R.I.P was typically an abbreviation for Rest in Peace, but in my case, it meant Resting in Provision. The demise of that brutal situationship forced me to see the big picture. By not allowing my courtships to prosper, God was making provisions for me, which would hopefully cancel out the mayhem of my past. My life had been going down a shame spiral ever since I had moved to ATL. It was time for me to start over. This time, I would let Jesus take the wheel because my GPS was broken. Every time I thought I was going in the right direction; life came out of nowhere and dropped the Reverse Uno card on me. At one point, I was so close to being ready for marriage that I could taste it. Unfortunately, the taste was bitter and lacked the nutrients that would have been able to sustain me. Formerly, I thought celibacy was the answer, but mischief still managed to follow me to sexless environments. Even while I was celibate, I was still so thirsty to find love that I would often drink

SITUATIONSHIP GURU | 113

from any and every well that I encountered. Not realizing that process was causing further dehydration, I continued to nourish the dry places of life with unhealthy relationships. Luckily, God always prevented me from getting in too deep to the point of no return. Recently, He had now allowed a professional athlete and a future celebrity R&B artist to slip from my grasp. At first, I was worried that I would never be able to find other men with such high status. I was falsely viewing them as the prize instead of realizing that I was indeed the ultimate reward. Once I realized who I was, I released all my fears and chose to trust God. My hands were now completely open to receive the blessing that God had for me, so I just knew He was about to hook me up. We were finally on the same page. Although my wants and His will didn't always align, I was beginning to understand His plan a little better. He didn't allow me to enter those meaningless relationships to try to hurt me. He was always trying to teach me to trust Him, no matter what. Now that I had learned the lessons, I assumed I would no longer be introduced to any more unfruitful relationships. Since I had finally passed the test, I expected God would send me my soul mate sooner rather than later.

GET YOUR EMOTIONS IN CHECK

Even though I was expecting God to send me His most eligible suitor, I was still a little hesitant to jump back into dating. Husbae had successfully shattered my confidence, and I was afraid to become emotionally intimate with anyone else. Premarital sex was a non-issue this time, but life's experiences had taught me that emotional connections were just as dangerous. My heart wasn't stable enough to take another hit, so I avoided all unnecessary male interaction. I refused to get it wrong this time, so if God wanted me to be with someone, He would need to make us run into each other. And that was what He did. While riding on the plane train at the Atlanta Hartsfield-Jackson Airport, I fell into the passenger beside me after the train came to an abrupt halt. I didn't have a type, but if I did, Abe would be it. He was the perfect mixture of melanin and muscles. Mesmerized by the handsome, tall, bearded man who had just broken my fall, I was temporarily left speechless.

"Sorry," was all that I could manage to whisper after several seconds of silence.

"No worries, beautiful. Now I can tell people this was the exact moment we fell in love," Abe chuckled.

The line was corny, but the huge smile on my face was evident that it still worked. Abe smiled back, causing me to blush a little. His teeth were glistening white. He looked like he had just finished filming a toothpaste commercial. Everything in me was attracted to him. From his perfectly shaped bald head to the Jordan's on his feet, he caught my attention. We spent a significant amount of time on the train, chatting, laughing, and smiling. We must have stopped at each terminal at least three times before I realized my flight was about to take off without me. I jumped off the plane train, scurried up the escalator, and dashed to my gate. As I sat in my seat, trying to catch my breath, I realized we never exchanged numbers. Heartbroken, I took a nap and tried to erase the fact that my potential life partner was now gone forever. Upon touching down at my destination, I received several social media alerts. It was him! He found me! And just like that, I went from feeling all hope was lost to a hopeless romantic. God must have had His hand in that. The Lord was looking out for me, strategically aligning my path with the person He had prepared for me.

Abe went on a liking spree on my social media page. He double-tapped every picture I had ever posted. It was very flattering, so I went to his page and returned the love. Upon viewing his page, I noticed "True Believer" was the first thing listed in his bio. I liked that. When I met him, he was rocking joggers and Jordan's, but several pictures of him in a suit were plastered all over his page. This man was pushing all my buttons in a good way. Abe sent me a direct message asking for my phone number. I desperately wanted to give him my digits, but I heard this still inner voice telling me to wait a while.

I wasn't sure why I had that feeling, but I had been fasting all week and was trying to be sensitive to all nudges. I feared Abe would dismiss me or think I was trying to play hard to get by not giving him my number, but he took it well. Once I explained to him that I wanted to get to know him a little better before giving him full access to me, he was on board with my decision. All my whirlwind relationships took a toll on me, so making Abe go through the vetting process was unavoidable. I wanted a long-term courtship that would eventually lead to a long-term commitment, marriage. Therefore, my only goal was to find out if he wanted the same thing. We talked about God, our goals, and areas for growth. We didn't talk much about past relationships, which was one hundred percent okay with me. I had no desire to relive my regrets. We did ensure each other that we had learned from our past mistakes and were both ready from something real. Every morning, I would wake up to a "Good Morning My Blessing" message from him in my inbox. In return, each night, I'd send him a "Kisses from the Misses" message. Our days began and ended with each other, so after about a month or so of quality assurance, I gave him my phone number.

Abe wasted no time hitting me up. He was thrilled that he had finally moved up a level on the leaderboard. He continually teased me about how I had kept him at arm's length for so long and that now that he had me, he'd be sure to keep me. We talked every night but hardly got to see each other. He was a truck driver for one of the major companies in Atlanta, so his schedule was almost impossible. It had been over a month since the last time we had seen each other, and we were both experiencing withdrawal symptoms. One day, Abe texted me while I was at work and requested to have a FaceTime date later that evening. I hurried home to apply a full face of makeup and change into a video-friendly outfit. The Facetime feature didn't have the filters that I often used on social media, so I piled on every piece of makeup I could find. He had seen me in person before, so he knew I wasn't a Catfish. However, all my IG pictures had been slightly, okay extremely altered, to enhance my natural beauty. Since he'd been forced to stare at the filtered pics and videos so long, he may have become accustomed to them. I prayed that he wouldn't be disappointed with the video chat, and more importantly when we finally got to see each other again.

BEING ATTRACTIVE ISN'T ENOUGH

My phone lit up, and so did the smile on my face. I had forgotten how attractive he was. Abe was ridiculously cute. He had every feature on the ill-guided list that I had written years ago, which contained the characteristics of the man I wanted to marry. Tall, beard, nice teeth, and from what I could remember, he also had big feet. Check, check, check, and a huge check mark to top it off. This materialistic list failed to include the more important qualities like God-fearing, patient, and kind. You know, all the things real love was made of.

Unfortunately, my list was just as immature as I was at the time. I hardly cared about the mental and spiritual stimulation that would be needed to sustain a successful, Godly relationship. Nope, I was letting my lust filled list do all the choosing. We were only on FaceTime for a few seconds before I suggested we just have a normal conversation. The physical attraction was overwhelming. I couldn't focus on anything he was saying. There was no way I could look into that beautiful face and carry on a meaningful conversation. We flirted expressing how attracted we were to one another and how the chemistry was strong. I could only imagine how much stronger it would be in person. The next day he suggested we try to FaceTime again. I had to prepare myself mentally to see that gorgeous face again. He was visually pleasing, but I was looking forward to learning more about who he was on the inside.

Once we began chatting, the conversation took an unwelcomed sexual turn. What started as compliments on my looks, quickly turned into Abe suggestively hinting for me to become his eye candy, so as he worded it, could "smooth one out." Deja vu! I had recently gone through that exact scenario with Husbae, except this time, I refused to participate. I disconnected the call immediately. Shortly after that, he sent me a text message saying that he was just joking with me. His excuse was not funny to me, nor did it make me feel comfortable about our future. Although I was overly attracted to him, I wanted our relationship to have a solid foundation. One that was not built solely on physical features.

UNCHANGED BEHAVIOR IS NOT AN ACCEPTABLE APOLOGY

The next day, my responses to him were cold and lacked the zeal they previously had. His *Good Morning* texts were usually reciprocated with pleasant salutations, followed by every love and kiss emoji known to man. But that day, a simple "Morning" followed by a period, sufficed. He could tell I was angry with him, so he tried to explain himself further. He realized his story about him just joking with me was getting him nowhere, so he changed his approach. Abe stated that he was just trying to express how attracted he was to me and didn't mean to be disrespectful.

He said, "When we have sex, it will be because you initiated it. I promise we can do everything at your pace."

That would've been the perfect opportunity to tell him that I was celibate and planned to stay that way until I was married, but I didn't.

I guess I was afraid that would cause him to leave immediately. Sex had been a huge part of my strategy to keep guys in the past. I wasn't quite sure how to introduce my celibacy into our relationship, so I hid that part of me from him. I figured God would provide an opportunity for me to share my truth when the time was right. In the meantime, I needed to figure out a way to maneuver around Abe's sexual comments. Anything sex- related was triggering for me, especially since I loved his looks. Continuing down that path would be dangerous. Falsely convincing myself that he was the person God had for me, I proceeded against my better judgment. Abe promised that he would never disrespect me again, and my dumb butt accepted his apology. We immediately picked back up where we left off with him showering me with compliments, and me flooding his texts with emojis. It felt good to be desired. Everything was going well until we decided to FaceTime again. A couple of minutes into the video chat, he began to indulge in more suggestive speech. At first, I didn't mind because who doesn't love a good compliment? But soon, his compliments were laced with sexual undertones that made me uncomfortable. The moment for me to tell him that I was saving it for marriage had come, but for some reason, I couldn't bring myself into saying it. I had been rejected too many times and didn't want to lose him for voicing the feelings that I was so desperately struggling to ignore. I desired him sexually as well but refused to expose myself to another soul tie. If I wanted the best of what God had for me, I would have to turn away from the things I used to do. I wanted God's will for my life, but I also wanted Abe in my life, so now it was time to choose. Abe was everything I thought I wanted, so I didn't want to give up that easily. In the middle of our conversation, I asked him if he remembered the promise, he had made to me, but he raised a voice a little and told me that I was killing his vibe. Less than two seconds later, I was face to face with his shaft. Yep, he went there! I immediately ended the video call. Well, not straight away. I did take a glance or two. What can I say? I'm human. But, after a few seconds, I hung up and blocked him.

It was over! What was it about me that screamed phone sex opera-
tor? Now I could understand how I was giving that vibe off in the past,
but now I was carrying myself differently and didn't understand why I
kept getting the same results. The old me would've given Abe a night
that he would never forget, but the new and improved me, did everything in my power to deny my flesh. It's like I was damned if I did and
damned if I didn't. I should've remained a hoe if the results would still
be the same. At least I would've gotten some temporary pleasure out
of the deal. This time I tried to do everything right and had nothing
to show for it. It wasn't fair. Why was God still punishing me? I didn't
have the answers to all the questions, but I did know one thing, God
needed to talk to me because I was sick of His games. We've all heard
the saying, "Your arms are too short to box with God", but I was willing to square up with Him that day. I hadn't had sex in several years,
and I wasn't refraining because I wanted to. I was doing it to please
God. I had suppressed all my sexual desires to be in the will of God, and
this is how He repaid me? I couldn't understand why He would dangle
my preferred vision in front of me just to snatch it away. When I first
moved to Atlanta, I bought a cute picture frame and placed it on my
nightstand. I had intentionally kept the frame blank because I planned
to put a picture of my future husband in the frame. I heard faith without
works is dead, but it seemed to me that I had wasted money to buy the
frame that was now still empty. Life was still empty. I was still empty.

SEEK WISE COUNSEL

Disappointment had become my new normal. Previously, I went on
a heart-felt rant about understanding God's plan for me. I went on and
on about how happy I was that I had passed the test and would never
have to retake it. Yet again, I found myself enrolled in another semester at the Believer's Academy, trying to figure out where I went wrong.

My situation required knowledge, knowledge that I either didn't have or didn't know how to use. No one had more wisdom than my grandmother, so I gave her a call, hoping that she could shed some light on my situation. She had been walking with God for most of the eighty plus years she had been on earth. She had seen it all and done it all before, so if anyone could break the scenarios down for me, it was she. With each failed relationship, I felt pulled further away from God. My Granny had a different point of view. She asked if I ever considered that He was using those situations to pull me toward Him, reminding me that the Bible says all things work together for our good. I understood where she was going, but honestly, it wasn't what I wanted to hear. She also suggested that every failed relationship, every tear I had cried, and every insecurity that I faced was just a piece of the puzzle. Granny reiterated that God is a mastermind and could take all the broken parts of my life and turn me into His masterpiece.

Then she asked me a question that I had been desperately trying to avoid, "Were there any red flags that you ignored before getting into these relationships?"

By the tone in her voice, I could tell she was getting ready to read me for filth. My Granny was old school and had mastered the art of telling it like is. Everything in me wanted to pretend to be naïve and convince her that I was the victim, but it was time that I faced my truth. She was aware of most of the other predicaments that I had been in, but we'd still be on the phone right now if I were to go down the laundry list of all my past lover's shortcomings. I swallowed my pride and disclosed only the red flags that I saw in Abe. Abe never took me a date, so that was the first sign that he didn't want to know me. When I asked him what he liked about me, he'd always either dodge the question or focus solely on physical attributes. If I was honest with myself, some of our initial conversations on social media revolved around sex. One time he sent me a risky meme where a woman was sitting on a man's lap, and he was whispering in her ear. Below the picture, he stated,

"This could be us, but you're playing." I didn't think anything of the picture at first. Especially since those are the type of things that couples do. But my longing to fulfill my physical meter allowed me to ignore the fact the woman in the picture was half- dressed, and the man had his hands placed on private areas of her body. He also suggested that we play "Never Have I Ever." Out of desperation to be liked by him, I convinced myself that he was just asking questions to get to know me. I let my loneliness overshadow the fact that most of his questions were raunchy. I couldn't see my Granny's face, but I assumed she was giving me the ultimate side- eye through the phone.

"God's trying to teach you discernment, but you're too dumb to get it!", she said.

Ouch! Granny did not take it easy on me at all. Her words hurt, but they were necessary. The fact that I had dated the same type of man multiple times meant something. They weren't the problem, I was. There was something about me, a defect in my character, that was attracting piss- poor men. If I didn't work toward my healing, I would continue down the same path for the rest of my life. The sad thing was, I thought I was already working on myself. I'd go to church more, take breaks from social media, and refrain from having sex, but my inner woman was still trash. I was beautiful on the outside, but my spirit was a dump truck full of unresolved issues. The men I attracted were a direct reflection on who I was on the inside. I had tried to convince everyone that just because I was celibate, I no longer struggled with sexual demons but that I was a lie. My body was technically pure but my thoughts and the websites I frequently visited when no one was looking, were not. I was the problem. Before letting me get off the phone to wallow in my pain, my Granny suggested that I read a familiar passage of scripture. Most of us are aware of the story of Adam and Eve. We all blame them for our demise. If it weren't for them, we would've all been in the Garden of Eden, butt naked and chilling. Life would've been good. Although I had read this story many times before, something spoke to my situation this time. Once again, Bible passages can sometimes be tricky, so I'll paraphrase Genesis 2: 18-23 below.

Adam and God were walking in the garden one day when Adam stopped to have a serious conversation with the Lord. "Can I keep it real with you?", Adam said. "What's realer than me?", God responded. "Okay so this garden is dope and everything but I'm getting a little lonely. Could you create someone for me, so I'll no longer feel alone?", Adam pleaded. "Say less.", the Lord replied. God went straight to work and started creating wild animals and birds. Then he brought them to Adam and told him to name them. Adam did as he was told but he was secretly a little confused. He specifically asked God to give him someone he could talk to, but God gave him a job instead. After God saw that Adam had fulfilled his purpose, he allowed him to get some rest. While Adam was sleeping, the Lord removed one of Adam's ribs and created Eve. Eve was so fine that Adam completely forgot about all the pain from the rib surgery he had just had. He recognized that Eve was the one he had been waiting for and he called her woman. They skipped the talking phase. They didn't care about each other's favorite color or which tv shows they were currently binge watching. Adam didn't make Eve suffer through an unnecessary situationship. He wifed her up immediately and they started living that newlywed life.

BEING ALONE CAN BE BENEFICIAL

God told Adam he shouldn't be alone in the eighteenth verse of the second chapter in Genesis. However, he didn't create Eve immediately after He made that statement. Instead, He made the animals first. I always wondered why God made animals before He made the woman, especially since He knew it wasn't good for a man to be alone. Later,

I realized that God was teaching Adam how to discern what was right for him and what wasn't. Adam named all the animals but didn't feel a connection with any of them, but as soon as he saw Eve, he knew she was the one for him. Maybe that is what God was doing for me. He was testing me and building discernment. God paraded Xavier, the unholy trinity, Husbae, and a bunch of other wild animals in front of me so that I could recognize frauds going forward. I should've been able to spot the liars and cheaters easily, but my inferiority complex clouded my judgment. I also realized that Adam had a purpose and knew who he was, so that was why he was able to identify Eve. She was a reflection of him. For me to receive the type of man that I wanted, I needed to become what I wanted first. Operation Walk in Purpose was now in full effect and would soon be my forever mission. It took several years for me to finally catch on and fall in line with God's plan. It was time for me to start over from the very beginning. God had placed me back in the Genesis phase of life and this time I was prepared. The antics of my past were a necessary part of my journey. To the men and women who participated in my various situationship history, I'd like to say thank you. You have taught me many valuable lessons, but now is the time for me to release you and wish you well. I'm proud to say that I am now an ex-situationship guru. No longer will I participate in toxic talking phases or fairy tale fauxmances.

FORGIVE AND MOVE FORWARD

I've always considered myself to be the female version of King David. I'm a woman after God's own heart, but my sexual appetite got me in trouble. I know I'm not the only woman that has used her yoni to cope with the woes of life, but despite my issues, I should have carried myself differently. Although I have since submitted my sinful sexual nature to the Lord, there are still a couple of areas in my life that are frowned upon by the super judgmental Christians. Now and then, I still enjoy a glass, okay, who am I kidding, a bottle of wine. Secular music is plastered throughout my active playlists. The dance floor has always been my happy place, so as soon as the beat drops, so do I. Afraid of being judged, I postponed writing this book for as long as I could. Yet, God kept pulling at me in various ways, encouraging me to finish the work that He started in me.

Like the woman with the issue of blood, and the woman at the well, I too had a problem only the Lord could resolve. Since you picked up this book, I have a feeling that we have a lot in common. Have you ever been rejected? Did a past relationship ever make you question your worth? Are your previous mistakes holding you back from living your best life? If you've answered yes to any of those questions or have found yourself trying to fill life's void with ungodly activities, please know that it's not too late to break free and live life abundantly. It is my hope that after hearing my story, you feel comfortable allowing God into the dark places of your life and trusting Him to deliver you from bondage. My journey from hoe to hallelujah wasn't easy, but it was worth it.

Throughout this excursion of my evolution, I've learned that there's nothing I can do to surprise God. God is not looking for us to be perfect. My story should be a clear reflection of that. He's just looking for our willingness to participate in His plans for us. So, here's what my participation looks like. It's me telling my story in hopes that someone else would be inspired to tell theirs. It's me not tampering with my truth in order to please others. Guilt is a purposeless emotion and is no longer welcomed in my life. God has already forgiven me, so it's only right that I forgive myself also. No longer will I be afraid of being authentic, nor will I be ashamed of my past. I now embrace every nook and cranny of my story, knowing that it has prepared me for a very dope future. If you feel the same, join me in the quick prayer.

GIVE IT TO GOD

Dear Heavenly Father, thank you dying for me in spite of my shortcomings. I appreciate you loving me and taking care of me when I couldn't properly care for myself. Please forgive me for my sins and help me to turn away from my trifling habits. I'm tired of trying to figure things out on my own, so I bring my past, present, and future mistakes to you. As I continue down this uncertain path called life, I am content that you will always be with me. Give me discernment to know who I should and shouldn't allow into my life. Allow me to see myself the way you see me and make me confident of who I am in You. In Jesus's name. Amen.

THE SIGNS ARE ALWAYS THERE

People don't just change overnight. They leave hints regarding their character from the very beginning, but sometimes we're too blinded by love to allow ourselves to see it. Other times, we treat the red flags as red carpets because we simply aren't ready to let them go yet. It's an unfortunate situation to deal with because we should never have mixed feelings about mixed signals. If someone really likes you, you'll know. You won't have to guess or decipher through a smorgasbord of words that are not accompanied by matching actions. If you are unclear as to whether or not the person likes you, just pay attention to what they aren't saying. Silence often speaks louder than words. Are they claiming you in public or just acting like y'all are cool? Do you know for a fact that you're the only person they are dealing with or is there evidence of a side piece? Remember, if you feel the need to ask "So what are we?" or "Where do you see this thing going?", you already have your answer. Ignoring the signs is the absolute worst thing you can do! If you've clearly stated your expectations of the relationship, yet they are trying to stick you in the talking phase maze, cut your losses and leave.

RELATIONSHIPS SHOULD BE PRIVATE, NOT SECRET

Social media has convinced us all that we need to share every single detail of our lives and that's simply not true. There are some things that should be sacred and only shared with loved ones; but your relationship status is not one of them. Although, it's beneficial to keep some aspects of your relationship private, don't ever let anyone keep you a secret! By definition, a secret is something that is kept or meant to be kept unknown or unseen by others. Who wants to be in a relationship that has to be kept in the dark? Secrecy is a sneaky and toxic trait that is destined to ruin relationships because it has negative effects on both parties. The person who is being kept a secret may began to feel insignificant. After several failed attempts to convince their boo to share their relationship status, they may begin to search for fulfillment outside the relationship. Similarly, since the general public is unaware of the secret keeper's relationship status, he or she may be approached with temptations that they are unable to flee from. I'm not saying secrecy always leads to cheating but that's exactly what happen in my case. Bottom line, your significant other shouldn't hide you, but instead, be proud to acknowledge the importance of having you in their life. If not, you need to change significant others. Simple.

SEX ONLY TEMPORARILY NUMBS THE PAIN

After experiencing that traumatic relationship, my only desire was to be desired. There were several times when I turned to sex just to make me feel better about myself. That was a very dangerous place to be in because late night rendezvous often turn into a lifetime of guilt and shame. During my sexual encounters, I would feel liberated and would experience a temporary high. Sex became my best friend and I depended on her to boost my self-esteem. It worked for a while, until I realized that instead of receiving fulfillment, I'd often leave the encounter feeling more empty than I was to begin with. Although I was no longer horny, I wasn't happy either. Learning that happiness can't be found at the bottom of an empty condom box was one of the best lessons that I ever received. It wasn't easy, but once I stopped self-medicating with lust, I began to see myself differently. Others began to see and treat me differently as well, which definitely feels better than cheap sex.

BEWARE OF COMFORT ZONES & COMFORT FOODS

Have you ever noticed that some of the foods with the sexiest packaging have of the worst ingredients? Most of our favorite go to snacks are filled with toxic artificial flavors. Just like food can be deceiving, certain people are completely void of value once you remove the package. What if people came with nutrition labels so you can really see what you're about to get yourself into? These labels would reveal the true traits of your potential mate, not just the convincing characteristics that their representative provides. Representatives often appear to have all the healthy ingredients but when you strip off the packaging, you'll realize that you're entertaining the equivalent of a processed tv dinner. So if we know this, why do we choose to allow our taste buds to lead us in the wrong direction? The answer is because it's comfortable. We run back to our dusty exes because the fauxmance provides us with something familiar. However, you should beware of comfort zones because familiarity doesn't mean the relationship is going to functioning properly.

WHEN SOMEONE GHOSTS YOU, DON'T TRY TO RESURRECT THEM

How many times has someone ghosted us and we grabbed our "pick me" shovels and tried to dig them up from the grave? When someone says, "I'm not looking for anything serious right now", why do we hear "Try Harder"? The worst possible thing we can do is try to change someone's mind about wanting to be with us. First of all, they should be grateful that our self-esteem dipped low enough for us to even look in their direction. Keep it real, if you were operating at your highest self, that person would have never been on your radar. But since you were bored, bitter or depressed, you let loneliness choose your lover. We attract who we are so instead of settling for situationships, level-up and date according to your worth. The next time someone exhibits signs that they don't want to be in a relationship with you, wish them well and keep it moving. Make them give you a title or make yourself un-available! Who has time to sit around waiting for someone to realize that you are a blessing? By the time they finally come to their senses, the price should have gone up and they need to put forth triple the effort to get your attention.

TAKE YOUR L LIKE A G

If you haven't noticed, I have a tendency to run from conflict instead of facing it head on. Whether it was avoiding closure or relocating when things got tricky, my dismissive nature often prevented me from properly working through my issues. Instead of running every time things got hard, I should have just taken my L like a G. Although it was painful to experience all those losses, I realized that the lessons I learned during my journey were extremely beneficial. Pastors often tell us that rejection can be God's protection. I can't believe I'm saying this, but a part of me is glad that I went through what I went through. Without those experiences, I wouldn't have been able to write this book and help those who have had similar experiences. And Lord forbid, I would have married any of the men I previously claimed to be so in love with. This book would have turned out quite different if God would have allowed me to get what I thought I wanted. From now on, the "G" in take your L like a G stands for God. Take Your L(oss) like a G(od) seems very befitting, especially since He's been using my L's to teach me how to become more like Him this whole time.

SEEK WISE COUNSEL

My Granny came through with a verbal body slam to help me realize just how off track my life was. It's very hard for me to admit when I need help so I'm thankful I have a trustworthy support system that I can confide in. If you're having relationship issues, seeking wise counsel is the best recommendation that I can give you. Talk to God, a counselor, trusted family members or get it popping in the friend group chat. When I was first experiencing relational trauma, I suffered in silence but you don't have to. There are people who care about you and are willing to help. All you have to do is ask. Lastly, I normally advise against taking relationship advice from single people, but you've already read my book so you might as well continue down this path with me. Plus, I won't be single forever (*Insert *"God I have seen what you've done for others"* prayer here). Similar to the book, my podcast outlines my journey from serial situationships to red flag connoisseur. Each episode is filled with tips and tricks on how to avoid fauxmances. Make sure you subscribe to The Ex-Situationship Guru podcast so you'll never miss any of my shenanigans.

ACKNOWLEDGEMENTS

It would be so awesome if I started this section like an old school church testimony service; "Giving Honor to God who is the head of my life." Seriously, although I go back and forth with God about just about everything, I'm glad that He never gave up on me. Even when I ran away from Him, His love continued to chase after me. For that, I am eternally grateful. I'd also like to thank my family and friends for supporting me throughout this adventure. Telling my testimony wasn't easy so I appreciate them for being my safe place. Lastly, I want to thank everyone who read this book. May you never be ashamed to be your authentic self. I pray that you live in peace and that God blesses you to be a blessing all the days of your life.

CPSIA information can be obtained
at www.ICGtesting.com
Printed in the USA
FSHW010951230321
79747FS

9 780578 855585